SONGS OF PRAISE
FOR CHILDREN

(FULL MUSIC EDITION)

Editors

P. DEARMER

R. VAUGHAN WILLIAMS

MARTIN SHAW

G. W. BRIGGS

*From ' Songs of Praise', with a few
additions from the ' Oxford Book
of Carols '*

GEOFFREY CUMBERLEGE
OXFORD UNIVERSITY PRESS
LONDON

Editions with Melody only

————

PRAYERS AND HYMNS FOR JUNIOR SCHOOLS
with SONGS OF PRAISE FOR CHILDREN

2s. 0d.

THE CHILDREN'S CHURCH
An Order of Morning and Evening Prayer,
with ' Songs of Praise for Children'.

2s. 6d.

————

OXFORD UNIVERSITY PRESS

PRINTED IN GREAT BRITAIN AT THE UNIVERSITY PRESS, OXFORD
BY CHARLES BATEY, PRINTER TO THE UNIVERSITY

PREFACE

EXPERIENCE has taught us to revise our standard of hymns for young people. Many so-called 'children's hymns' were not hymns which children liked, but hymns which grown-up people thought that children ought to like; and in the end it has transpired that the young folk are not so unsophisticated, and really enjoy the best of the 'grown-up' hymns. It is, of course, true that there are a few hymns unsuitable for adults, but suitable for children; and they must be included in a children's hymn-book. It is equally true that there are some hymns (as for instance 'Lead, kindly Light' or 'Abide with me') which are suitable for adults, but would be unreal on the lips of children; and for that reason they have been omitted. But no rigid line can be drawn between hymns for the young and hymns for older people; and, generally speaking, the sooner young people learn the hymns which will last them all their life, the better for them.

There is one advantage which young people possess: they start with fresh minds, and are prepared to judge a hymn on its merits, and not on their own association, or lack of association. Nor are they afraid of experiment. It has been proved by enthusiastic teachers that even young children are capable of singing tunes which seem at first sight fairly difficult; and it has been found that part-singing is by no means beyond them. For that reason there are a number of descants in this book; and one hymn—a School Anniversary hymn, where the special pains may seem more than usually justified—is written in three parts.

The inclusion of Carols will undoubtedly be popular. It was necessary to limit their number; and some familiar favourites (like 'The First Nowell') were reluctantly left out. But these are already easily available; a very complete selection may be found in the *Oxford Book of Carols* (Oxford University Press).

Singing, like speech, should be as natural as possible; and, in appearance at any rate, spontaneous. In appearance, because behind any real perfection there is the effort of true art. But the art must not obtrude itself: *ars est celare artem*. Rigidity kills singing, as it kills most things. In this book breathing-spaces and rests are noted, not in order to impose fetters, but to give freedom: the rests need not always be of the same length. The modern habit is to sing too fast: the tendency to 'drawl' is too often corrected by a breathless gallop. But that is a counsel of despair: we must learn the art of singing without hurry, yet without 'drawling'. There is a natural instinct which tells most people the pace at which they can sing with comfort. That pace varies with the singers, with their number, and with the size and acoustic properties of the building; and it is the art of the wise instructor to take all these into consideration. The natural instinct of the singers needs training and constant guidance; but to force it into a rigid mould is disastrous.

It is generally agreed that a revival of singing is of first-rate educational importance. Our national tendency to self-depreciation—even though some might call it the reflex action of our national self-assertiveness—is to regard ourselves as an unmusical people. But the fact remains that we have a great musical inheritance; and it is surely well worth recovering.

ACKNOWLEDGEMENTS

THANKS are due to the following copyright owners for permission to include hymns and tunes:

HYMNS

Miss E. Alexander (p. 209); Very Rev. Dr. C. A. Alington, 57; Messrs. Boosey & Co., Ltd., and Mr. Norman Gale, 67; Mr. H. N. Brailsford, 16; Rev. Canon G. W. Briggs, 7, 20, 83, 95, 145, Grace 1, Friday I (p. 205); Miss Honor Brooke, 30; Professor F. C. Burkitt and S.P.C.K., 61; Messrs. J. Curwen & Sons, Ltd., 14 (from Curwen Edition No. 6333); Rev. Dr. Dearmer, 33, 74, 81, 114, 129; the Proprietors of *The English Hymnal*, 39, 45, 68; Miss Eleanor Farjeon, 134; Mr. William Galbraith, 5; Mr. Norman Gale and Messrs. Boosey & Co., Ltd., 67; Mrs. Maxtone Graham, 48, 73, 96, 101, 105, 132, Carol 10; Miss Beatrice Hatch, 80; Mr. R. Holland, 144; Houghton Mifflin Company, 70; Mr. F. D. How, 97; Mr. Rudyard Kipling, 148 (from *Puck of Pook's Hill*, published by Messrs. Macmillan & Co., Ltd.); Mrs. E. Rutter Leatham, Grace 2; The Head Master, The Grammar School, Loughborough, and the Head Mistress of Loughborough High School, 145; Mr. Basil Mathews, 124; Estate of the late Mr. Thomas B. Mosher, 103; Mrs. Myers, 76; Oxford University Press, 7, 20, 36, 48, 73, 83, 95, 96, 101, 105, 132, Carol 10, Friday I (p. 205); Rev. W. Charter Piggott, 65, 71, 88; Miss M. F. Pott, 58; Messrs. A. W. Ridley & Co., 79, 128, 140; Mr. W. H. C. Romanis, 141; Society for Promoting Christian Knowledge, 61; Mr. L. G. P. Thring, 125; also from the *Yattendon Hymnal*, 64, 109, 143.

We also acknowledge the copyright hymns under the initials, A. F., E. H., N. S. T., O. B. C., S. P., S. P. V.; also the centos and versions marked † or ‡.

TUNES

(The numbers marked with an asterisk denote a Fa-burden or Descant Version.)

Mr. J. H. Arnold (p. 214); Miss N. M. Bicknell, 51; Rev. Canon G. W. Briggs, 14, 95, 145, Amens ii, iii, Monday I (p. 192), pp. 212–13; Rev. Canon G. W. Briggs and Dr. Gordon Slater, Monday II (p. 193), Thursday I (pp. 199–202), p. 216; Messrs. J. Curwen & Sons, Ltd., from Curwen Editions Nos. 6300: 22*, 29, 79, 89, 91, 126; 8606: 108; 71655: 18; 80629: 15; 80635: 43*; Chants Nos. 2 and 3, p. 217, from Curwen Edition No. 6352; the Proprietors of *The English Hymnal*, 28 (har.), 87, 88 (har.), 147; Dr. David Evans, p. 208; The Faith Press, Ltd., 24*, 86*, 127*, from *The Tenor Tune Book*; Mr. K. G. Finlay, 101; Mr. W. Greatorex, 124; Mr. Patrick Harvey, 53*; Mr. Gustav Holst, 18, 128; Messrs. Hughes & Son, 31; Miss Maud Karpeles, 92, 132, 144; Dr. Henry G. Ley, 57 (har.); Messrs. A. R. Mowbray & Co., Ltd., Carol 8; Messrs. Novello & Co., Ltd., 42; from the *Oxford Book of Carols*, Carols 1–7, 9, 10; Oxford University Press, 2, 14, 19, 20, 33, 36,

53*, 57 (har.), 95, 103, 106 (har.), 137, 145, Monday I (p. 192), p. 211; Messrs. A. W. Ridley & Co., 140; Miss Evelyn Sharpe, 19, 33; Dr. Geoffrey Shaw, 62 (har.), 102, 103, 142 (har.); Dr. Martin Shaw and Oxford University Press, 2, 14*, 36, 145*, Tuesday I (pp. 194–5), Thursday II (pp. 204–5), Friday II (p. 206), p. 210, pp. 212–13* ; Dr. Gordon Slater, 20, Amen vii, Amen, p. 193, Wednesday I, p. 197, Service for any Day, p. 207; Sir Arthur Somervell, p. 211; Messrs. Stainer & Bell, Ltd., 26 (har.), p. 209 ; the Musical Editors of *Songs of Praise* (Dr. R. Vaughan Williams and Dr. Martin Shaw), 7*, 17 (har.), 37, 44, 45, 61, 67, 68, 71, 72, 73, 74, 77, 83, 96 (har.), 97, 105 (har.), 113, 129, 133 (har.), 134, 135, 136*, Carols, 2, 3, 4, 7, 10, Friday I (p. 205); the Editors of *A Students' Hymnal*, 30; Dr. J. Lloyd Williams, 17 (melody); Dr. R. Vaughan Williams, Amen vi, Tuesday II (p. 196), Wednesday II (p. 198); Thursday I (page 203); Rev. Canon David F. R. Wilson, 115 (har.).

CONTENTS

NOTES

Where it is desired to shorten hymns, verses marked with an asterisk may be omitted.

For the youngest children, who may not yet be quick at reading unfamiliar phrases, it may be desirable, until the words are familiar, to omit verses in other hymns. But circumstances vary so much, that it must be left entirely to the discretion of the teacher.

In making any omission, care should be taken to preserve, as far as possible, the unity and sequence of the hymn.

'Amen' is only printed in special cases. Its proper use is after a doxology; and its indiscriminate use obscures its meaning.

SUGGESTIONS FOR SINGING

1. As far as possible, breathe only once for each line of the words.

2. Avoid sudden contrasts of soft and loud. Of course, certain verses may be sung softly, and others more loudly, but generally keep to a broad and even medium tone.

3. Articulate the consonants distinctly, particularly at the beginnings of words.

4. In every line there is generally some predominating word. This may be sung with more significance or even strength, giving variety to the performance. It will add interest to the practice if the class be asked to suggest such word.

Sometimes a word is unfamiliar; or a phrase, though easily understood when explained, will convey no meaning, or else a meaning which is not intended. A few simple questions will often receive some surprising answers; and an occasional exposition of a hymn, as of a prayer, will clear away many wrong conceptions, which may survive long after school-days.

HYMNS

GOD OUR FATHER

OLD HUNDREDTH. (L.M.)

Slow and dignified.

Melody from *Genevan Psalter*, 1551.
(English form of final line.)

Ps. 100.   *W. Kethe, Daye's Psalter (1560–1). Scottish Psalter (1650) version.*

ALL people that on earth do dwell,
  Sing to the Lord with cheerful voice;
Him serve with mirth, his praise forth tell,
  Come ye before him, and rejoice.

2 The Lord, ye know, is God indeed,
  Without our aid he did us make;
We are his folk, he doth us feed,
  And for his sheep he doth us take.

3 O enter then his gates with praise;
  Approach with joy his courts unto,
Praise, laud, and bless his name always,
  For it is seemly so to do.

4 For why? the Lord our God is good:
  His mercy is for ever sure,
His truth at all times firmly stood,
  And shall from age to age endure.

5 To Father, Son, and Holy Ghost,
  The God whom heaven and earth adore,
From men and from the angel-host
  Be praise and glory evermore.

I *(cont.)* ALTERNATIVE VERSION (for verses 2 and 4).

MELODY.

Fa-burden by J. DOWLAND, 1562–1626.

DESCANT.

NOTE.—*This alternative version may be used in connexion with the first for these two verses, half the voices singing the melody as usual.*

Ps. 100.   *W. Kethe, Daye's Psalter* (1560–1), *and Scottish Psalter* (1650).

ALL people that on earth do dwell,
  Sing to the Lord with cheerful voice;
Him serve with mirth, his praise forth tell,
  Come ye before him, and rejoice.

(Descant) 2 The Lord, ye know, is God indeed;
  Without our aid he did us make;
We are his folk, he doth us feed,
  And for his sheep he doth us take.

3 O enter then his gates with praise;
  Approach with joy his courts unto;
Praise, laud, and bless his name always,
  For it is seemly so to do.

(Descant) 4 For why? the Lord our God is good:
  His mercy is for ever sure,
His truth at all times firmly stood,
  And shall from age to age endure.

5 To Father, Son, and Holy Ghost,
  The God whom heaven and earth adore,
From men and from the angel-host
  Be praise and glory evermore.

A - men.

2

GUN HILL. (5 5. 6 5. 8 7. 8 7.)
In moderate time.

MARTIN SHAW.

[*Copyright, 1929, by Oxford University Press.*]

S. P. from Goethe.

EVERYTHING changes,
But God changes not;
The power never changes
That lies in his thought:
Splendours three, from God proceeding,
May we ever love them true,
Goodness, Truth, and Beauty heeding
Every day, in all we do.

2 Truth never changes,
And Beauty's her dress,
And Good never changes,
Which those two express:

3 Perfect together
And lovely apart,
These three cannot wither;
They spring from God's heart:

4 Some things are screening
God's glory below;
But this is the meaning
Of all that we know:

(4)

3

NICAEA. (11 12. 12 10.)   J. B. DYKES, 1823–76.

NOTE.—*This hymn is marked to be sung at a much slower rate than usual: it may, if preferred, be sung at the more usual rate of ♩ = 63 and the pauses may be omitted.*

Bishop R. Heber, 1783–1826.

HOLY, Holy, Holy! Lord God Almighty!
    Early in the morning our song shall rise to thee;
Holy, Holy, Holy! Merciful and mighty!
    God in three Persons, blessèd Trinity!

2 Holy, Holy, Holy! all the Saints adore thee,
    Casting down their golden crowns around the glassy sea;
Cherubim and Seraphim falling down before thee,
    Which wert, and art, and evermore shalt be.

3 Holy, Holy, Holy! though the darkness hide thee,
    Though the eye of sinful man thy glory may not see,
Only thou art holy, there is none beside thee
    Perfect in power, in love, and purity.

4 Holy, Holy, Holy! Lord God Almighty!
    All thy works shall praise thy name, in earth, and sky, and sea;
Holy, Holy, Holy! Merciful and mighty!
    God in three Persons, blessèd Trinity!

4

OLD 137TH. (D.C.M.)
Moderately slow.

Day's Psalter, 1563.

John Mason, c. 1645–94.

HOW shall I sing that majesty
  Which angels do admire?
Let dust in dust and silence lie;
  Sing, sing, ye heavenly choir.
Thousands of thousands stand around
  Thy throne, O God most high;
Ten thousand times ten thousand sound
  Thy praise; but who am I?

2 Thy brightness unto them appears,
  Whilst I thy footsteps trace;
A sound of God comes to my ears,
  But they behold thy face.
They sing because thou art their sun;
  Lord, send a beam on me;
For where heaven is but once begun
  There alleluyas be.

3 Enlighten with faith's light my heart,
  Inflame it with love's fire;
Then shall I sing and bear a part
  With that celestial choir.
I shall, I fear, be dark and cold,
  With all my fire and light;
Yet when thou dost accept their gold,
  Lord, treasure up my mite.

4 How great a being, Lord, is thine,
  Which doth all beings keep!
Thy knowledge is the only line
  To sound so vast a deep.
Thou art a sea without a shore,
  A sun without a sphere;
Thy time is now and evermore,
  Thy place is everywhere.

5

ST. DENIO. (11 11. 11 11.)
In moderate time.

Welsh Hymn Melody.

W. Chalmers Smith, 1824–1908.

IMMORTAL, invisible, God only wise,
    In light inaccessible hid from our eyes,
Most blessèd, most glorious, the ancient of days,
Almighty, victorious, thy great name we praise.

2 Unresting, unhasting, and silent as light,
    Nor wanting, nor wasting, thou rulest in might;
    Thy justice like mountains high soaring above,
    Thy clouds which are fountains of goodness and love.

3 To all life thou givest, to both great and small;
    In all life thou livest, the true life of all;
    We blossom and flourish as leaves on the tree,
    And wither and perish; but nought changeth thee.

4 Great Father of glory, pure Father of light,
    Thine angels adore thee, all veiling their sight;
    All laud we would render: O help us to see
    'Tis only the splendour of light hideth thee.

(7)

6

WESTMINSTER. (C.M.)
In moderate time.
J. TURLE, 1802–82.

F. W. Faber,‡ 1814–63.

MY God, how wonderful thou art,
  Thy majesty how bright,
How beautiful thy mercy-seat,
  In depths of burning light!

2 How dread are thine eternal years,
  O everlasting Lord,
By shining spirits day and night
  Incessantly adored!

3 Yet I may love thee too, O Lord,
  Almighty as thou art,
For thou hast stooped to ask of me
  The love of my poor heart.

4 No earthly father loves like thee,
  No mother, e'er so mild,
Bears and forbears as thou hast done
  With me thy wilful child.

5 How wonderful, how beautiful,
  The sight of thee must be,
Thine endless wisdom, boundless power,
  And aweful purity!

7

FARRANT. (C.M.)

Rather slow.   Adapted from an Anthem of the school of R. FARRANT, *c.* 1530-80.

ALTERNATIVE VERSION

DESCANT.   MARTIN SHAW.

[*Copyright, 1931, by Martin Shaw.*]

The Abiding Presence.   G. W. Briggs.

O GOD, in whom we live and move,
In whom we draw each breath,
Who fillest all the height above,
And all the depths beneath;

(*Descant*) 2 Our hands may build thy hallowed fane,
No bound thy presence owns;
The heaven of heavens cannot contain,
The lowly heart enthrones.

3 Thou art about our path, where'er
We seek to tread thy ways;
All life is sacrament and prayer,
And every thought is praise.

GOD OUR FATHER

8

LAUDATE DOMINUM. (5 5. 5 5. 6 5. 6 5.)
Moderately slow.

H. J. GAUNTLETT, 1805-76.
(first four bars reharmonized.)

Ps. 150.

Sir H. W. Baker, 1821-77.

O PRAISE ye the Lord!
   Praise him in the height;
Rejoice in his word,
   Ye angels of light;
Ye heavens, adore him
   By whom ye were made,
And worship before him,
   In brightness arrayed.

2 O praise ye the Lord!
   Praise him upon earth,
In tuneful accord,
   Ye sons of new birth;
Praise him who hath brought you
   His grace from above,
Praise him who hath taught you
   To sing of his love.

3 O praise ye the Lord,
   All things that give sound;
Each jubilant chord,
   Re-echo around;
Loud organs, his glory
   Forth tell in deep tone,
And sweet harp, the story
   Of what he hath done.

4 O praise ye the Lord!
   Thanksgiving and song
To him be outpoured
   All ages along:
For love in creation,
   For heaven restored,
For grace of salvation,
   O praise ye the Lord!

9

HANOVER. (5 5. 5 5. 6 5. 6 5.)
Slow.

Probably by W. CROFT, 1678-1727.

Ps. 104.　　　　　　　　　　　　　　　　　*Sir R. Grant,‡* 1785–1838.

O WORSHIP the King
　　All glorious above;
O gratefully sing
　　His power and his love:
Our shield and defender,
　　The Ancient of Days,
Pavilioned in splendour,
　　And girded with praise.

2 O tell of his might,
　　O sing of his grace,
Whose robe is the light,
　　Whose canopy space.
His chariots of wrath
　　The deep thunder-clouds form,
And dark is his path
　　On the wings of the storm.

3 This earth, with its store
　　Of wonders untold,
Almighty, thy power
　　Hath founded of old:
Hath stablished it fast
　　By a changeless decree,
And round it hath cast,
　　Like a mantle, the sea.

4 Thy bountiful care
　　What tongue can recite?
It breathes in the air,
　　It shines in the light;
It streams from the hills,
　　It descends to the plain,
And sweetly distils
　　In the dew and the rain.

*5 Frail children of dust,
　　And feeble as frail,
In thee do we trust,
　　Nor find thee to fail;
Thy mercies how tender!
　　How firm to the end!—
Our Maker, Defender,
　　Redeemer, and Friend!

6 O measureless Might,
　　Ineffable Love,
While angels delight
　　To hymn thee above,
Thy humbler creation,
　　Though feeble their lays,
With true adoration
　　Shall sing to thy praise.

IO

AUSTRIAN HYMN. (8 7. 8 7. D.)
Moderately slow.

F. J. HAYDN, 1732–1809.

Ps. 148.

Foundling Hospital Coll. (1796).

PRAISE the Lord! ye heavens, adore him;
   Praise him, Angels, in the height;
Sun and moon, rejoice before him,
   Praise him, all ye stars and light:
Praise the Lord! for he hath spoken,
   Worlds his mighty voice obeyed;
Laws, which never shall be broken,
   For their guidance hath he made.

2 Praise the Lord! for he is glorious;
   Never shall his promise fail;
God hath made his saints victorious,
   Sin and death shall not prevail.
Praise the God of our salvation;
   Hosts on high, his power proclaim;
Heaven and earth, and all creation,
   Laud and magnify his name!

II

LOBE DEN HERREN. (14 14. 4. 7. 8.)

Moderately slow.

Later form of melody in *Stralsund Gesangbuch,* 1665
(as given in *The Chorale Book for England,* 1863).

J. Neander, 1650–80. *Tr. C. Winkworth, S.P.V.*

Lobe den Herren.

PRAISE to the Lord, the Almighty,
 the King of creation;
O my soul, praise him, for he is thy
 health and salvation:
  Come, ye who hear,
  Brothers and sisters, draw near,
Praise him in glad adoration.

2 Praise to the Lord, who o'er all things
 so wondrously reigneth,
Shelters thee under his wings, yea, so
 gently sustaineth:
  Hast thou not seen?
  All that is needful hath been
Granted in what he ordaineth.

3 Praise to the Lord, who doth prosper
 thy work and defend thee;
Surely his goodness and mercy here
 daily attend thee:
  Ponder anew
  All the Almighty can do,
He who with love doth befriend thee.

4 Praise to the Lord! O let all that is in
 me adore him!
All that hath life and breath come now
 with praises before him!
  Let the amen
  Sound from his people again:
Gladly for ay we adore him!

12

CROFT'S 136TH. (6 6. 6 6. 8 8.)
In moderate time.

W. CROFT, 1678–1727.

Ps. 148.

George Wither, 1588–1667.

THE Lord of Heaven confess;
　　On high his glory raise:
Him let all angels bless,
　Him all his armies praise.
　　　Him glorify
　　　　Sun, moon, and stars;
　　　　Ye higher spheres,
　　　And cloudy sky.

2 Praise God from earth below,
　　Ye dragons, and ye deeps,
Fire, hail, clouds, wind, and snow,
　Whom in command he keeps.
　　　Praise ye his name,
　　　　Hills great and small,
　　　　Trees low and tall,
　　　Beasts wild and tame.

3 O let God's name be praised
　　Above both earth and sky;
For he his saints hath raised,
　And set their horn on high;
　　　Yea, they that are
　　　　Of Israel's race,
　　　　Are in his grace
　　　And ever dear.

(14)

13

LLANSANNAN. (8 7. 8 7. D.)

In moderate time, dignified.

Welsh Hymn Melody.

F. W. Faber, 1814–63.

THERE'S a wideness in God's
  mercy
Like the wideness of the sea;
There's a kindness in his justice
  Which is more than liberty.
There is no place where earth's sorrows
  Are more felt than up in heaven;
There is no place where earth's failings
  Have such kindly judgment given.

2 There is grace enough for thousands
  Of new worlds as great as this;
There is room for fresh creations
  In that upper home of bliss.
For the love of God is broader
  Than the measures of man's mind;
And the heart of the Eternal
  Is most wonderfully kind:

3 But we make his love too narrow
  By false limits of our own;
And we magnify his strictness
  With a zeal he will not own.
If our love were but more simple,
  We should take him at his word;
And our lives would be all sunshine
  In the sweetness of our Lord.

GOD OUR FATHER

14

ST. FRANCIS. (8 8. 4 4. 8 8, and Alleluyas.)

Brightly.

G. W. BRIGGS.

A - men.

poco rall.

GOD OUR FATHER

Optional Descant for vv. 2 and 4. (Accompaniment as before.)   MARTIN SHAW.

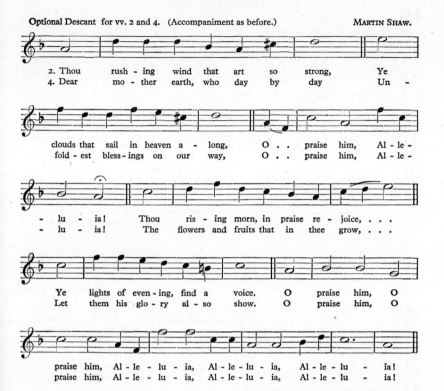

2. Thou rush-ing wind that art so strong, Ye
4. Dear mo-ther earth, who day by day Un -

clouds that sail in heaven a - long, O . . praise him, Al - le -
fold-est bless-ings on our way, O . . praise him, Al - le -

- lu - ia! Thou ris - ing morn, in praise re - joice, . . .
- lu - ia! The flowers and fruits that in thee grow, . . .

Ye lights of even-ing, find a voice. O praise him, O
Let them his glo - ry al - so show. O praise him, O

praise him, Al - le - lu - ia, Al - le - lu - ia, Al - le - lu - ia!
praise him, Al - le - lu - ia, Al - le - lu - ia, Al - le - lu - ia!

W. H. Draper, based on St. Francis.

ALL creatures of our God and King,
Lift up your voice and with us sing
Alleluia, Alleluia!
Thou burning sun with golden beam,
Thou silver moon with softer gleam,
O praise him, O praise him,
Alleluia, Alleluia, Alleluia!

2 *Thou rushing wind that art so strong,*
Ye clouds that sail in heaven along,
O praise him, Alleluia!
Thou rising morn, in praise rejoice,
Ye lights of evening, find a voice.
O praise him, O praise him,
Alleluia, Alleluia, Alleluia!

3 *Thou flowing water, pure and clear,*
Make music for thy Lord to hear,
Alleluia, Alleluia!
Thou fire so masterful and bright,

That givest man both warmth and light,
O praise him, O praise him,
Alleluia, Alleluia, Alleluia!

4 *Dear mother earth, who day by day*
Unfoldest blessings on our way,
O praise him, Alleluia!
The flowers and fruits that in thee grow,
Let them his glory also show.
O praise him, O praise him,
Alleluia, Alleluia, Alleluia!

5 Let all things their Creator bless,
And worship him in humbleness,
O praise him, Alleluia!
Praise, praise the Father, praise the Son,
And praise the Spirit, Three in One.
O praise him, O praise him,
Alleluia, Alleluia, Alleluia! Amen.

(NOTE.—*The parts in italics may be sung by a semi-chorus, all joining in the refrains; except when the descant is sung.*)

15

ROYAL OAK. (7 6. 7 6, and refrain.)

Fast.

Adapted from an English Traditional
Melody by MARTIN SHAW.

1. *All things bright and beau - ti - ful, All crea - tures great and small, All things wise and won - der - ful, The Lord God made them all.* 2. *Each lit - tle flower that*

FINE.

o - pens, Each lit - tle bird that sings, He

D.C.

made their glow - ing col - ours, He made their ti - ny wings:

NOTE.—*The pause (⌒) is for the last time only.*

Mrs. C. F. Alexander,‡ 1823–95.

ALL things bright and beautiful,
All creatures great and small,
All things wise and wonderful,
The Lord God made them all.

2 Each little flower that opens,
   Each little bird that sings,
   He made their glowing colours,
   He made their tiny wings:

3 The purple-headed mountain,
   The river running by,
   The sunset and the morning,
   That brightens up the sky:

4 The cold wind in the winter,
   The pleasant summer sun,
   The ripe fruits in the garden,
   He made them every one:

5 The tall trees in the greenwood,
   The meadows for our play,
   The rushes by the water
   To gather every day:

6 He gave us eyes to see them,
   And lips that we might tell
   How great is God Almighty,
   Who has made all things well:

JACKSON. (C.M.)
In moderate time.

T. JACKSON, 1715–81.

Edward J. Brailsford, 1841–1921.

Aᴸᴸ things which live below the sky,
Or move within the sea,
Are creatures of the Lord most high,
And brothers unto me.

2 I love to hear the robin sing,
Perched on the highest bough;
To see the rook with purple wing
Follow the shining plough.

3 I love to watch the swallow skim
The river in his flight;
To mark, when day is growing dim,
The glow-worm's silvery light;

4 The sea-gull whiter than the foam,
The fish that dart beneath;
The lowing cattle coming home;
The goats upon the heath.

5*God taught the wren to build her nest,
The lark to soar above,
The hen to gather to her breast
The offspring of her love.

6*Beneath his heaven there's room for all;
He gives to all their meat;
He sees the meanest sparrow fall
Unnoticed in the street.

7 Almighty Father, King of Kings,
The lover of the meek,
Make me a friend of helpless things,
Defender of the weak.

17

TREFAENAN. (8 7. 8 7. 8 8. 8 7.)
Not too quick.

Welsh Traditional Melody.

He hath made them, He hath made them, He hath made them, ev - 'ry one.
And he loves them, And he loves them, And he loves them, ev - 'ry one.

Johann W. Hey (1837). *Tr. H. W. Dulcken.*

Weisst du wie viel Sternlein.

CAN you count the stars that brightly
Twinkle in the midnight sky?
Can you count the clouds, so lightly
O'er the meadows floating by?
God, the Lord, doth mark their number
With his eyes that never slumber;
He hath made them, every one.

2 Do you know how many children
Rise each morning blithe and gay?
Can you count their jolly voices,
Singing sweetly day by day?
God hears all the happy voices,
In their pretty songs rejoices;
And he loves them, every one.

18

THEODORIC. (6 6 6. 6 6. 5 5. 3. 9.)

In moderate time.

Melody from *Piae Cantiones*, 1582.
Arranged by GUSTAV HOLST.

1. God is love: his the care,
Tend-ing each, ev-'ry-where. God is love— all is there!
Je-sus came to show him, That man-kind might know him:

GOD OUR FATHER

Sing a - loud, loud, loud! Sing a - loud, loud, loud!

God is good! God is truth! God is beau - ty! Praise him!

A. F.

GOD is love: his the care,
Tending each, everywhere.
God is love—all is there!
    Jesus came to show him,
    That mankind might know him:

Sing aloud, loud, loud!
Sing aloud, loud, loud!
God is good!
God is truth! God is beauty! Praise him!

2 None can see God above;
All have here man to love;
Thus may we Godward move,
    Finding him in others,
    Holding all men brothers:

3 Jesus lived here for men,
Strove and died, rose again,
Rules our hearts, now as then;
    For he came to save us
    By the truth he gave us:

*4 To our Lord praise we sing—
Light and life, friend and king,
Coming down love to bring,
    Pattern for our duty,
    Showing God in beauty:

(23)

GOD OUR FATHER

19

PLATT'S LANE. (5 6. 6 4.)

In moderate time.

EVELYN SHARPE.

[*Copyright, 1929, by Oxford University Press.*]

Sarah Betts Rhodes (1870).

GOD who made the earth,
　The air, the sky, the sea,
Who gave the light its birth,
　Careth for me.

2 God, who made the grass,
　　The flower, the fruit, the tree,
　The day and night to pass,
　　Careth for me.

3 God who made the sun,
　　The moon, the stars, is he
　Who, when life's clouds come on,
　　Careth for me.

(24)

BILSDALE. (D.C.M. Irreg.)

In moderate time.

GORDON SLATER.

[*Copyright, 1931, by Oxford University Press.*]

G. W. Briggs.

I LOVE God's tiny creatures
    That wander wild and free,
The coral-coated lady-bird,
    The velvet humming-bee;
Shy little flowers in hedge and dyke
    That hide themselves away:
God paints them, though they are so small,
    God makes them bright and gay.

2 Dear Father, who hast all things made,
    And carest for them all,
There 's none too great for thy great love,
    Nor anything too small:
If thou canst spend such tender care
    On things that grow so wild,
How wonderful thy love must be
    For me, thy loving child.

21

NUN DANKET. (6 7. 6 7. 6 6. 6 6.)

Slow and majestic.

Present form of melody by J. CRÜGER, 1598–1662.

A-men.

M. Rinkart, 1586–1649. Tr. C. Winkworth.

Nun danket alle Gott.

NOW thank we all our God,
  With heart and hands and voices,
Who wondrous things hath done,
In whom his world rejoices;
  Who from our mother's arms
    Hath blessed us on our way
With countless gifts of love,
    And still is ours to-day.

2   O may this bounteous God
Through all our life be near us,
  With ever joyful hearts
And blessèd peace to cheer us,
  And keep us in his grace,
    And guide us when perplexed,
  And free us from all ills
    In this world and the next.

3   All praise and thanks to God
The Father now be given,
  The Son, and him who reigns
With them in highest heaven,
  The one eternal God,
    Whom earth and heaven adore;
  For thus it was, is now,
    And shall be evermore.   Amen.

22

ST. ANNE. (C.M.)
Slow and dignified.

Melody from the *Supplement to the New Version*, 1708.
Probably by W. CROFT, 1678–1727.

ALTERNATIVE VERSION (for verses 3 and 5).

Melody in the Tenor.

Fa-burden by MARTIN SHAW.

[*Copyright*, 1915, by *J. Curwen & Sons, Ltd.*]

Ps. 90.

I. Watts, 1674–1748.

O GOD, our help in ages past,
  Our hope for years to come,
Our shelter from the stormy blast,
  And our eternal home;

2 Under the shadow of thy throne
  Thy saints have dwelt secure;
Sufficient is thine arm alone,
  And our defence is sure.

3 Before the hills in order stood,
  Or earth received her frame,
From everlasting thou art God,
  To endless years the same.

4 A thousand ages in thy sight
  Are like an evening gone,
Short as the watch that ends the night
  Before the rising sun.

5 Time, like an ever-rolling stream,
  Bears all its sons away;
They fly forgotten, as a dream
  Dies at the opening day.

6. O God, our help in ages past,
  Our hope for years to come,
Be thou our guard while troubles last,
  And our eternal home.

(28)

PRAISE, MY SOUL.* (8 7. 8 7. 8 7.)

In moderate time.

J. Goss, 1800–80.

1. Praise, my soul, the King of hea - ven; To his feet thy tri - bute bring.

Ransom'd, heal'd, re-stor'd, for - giv - en, Who like me his praise should sing?

Praise him! Praise him! Praise him! Praise him! Praise the ev - er - last - ing King.

(See overleaf.)

* *If desired, the music of verse 2 may be used for the hymn throughout.*

23 (*continued*)

2. Praise him for his grace and fa - - vour To our fa - thers
3. Fa - ther - like, he tends and spares us; Well our fee - ble

in dis - tress; Praise him still the same for ev - er,
frame he knows; In his hands he gen - tly bears us,

Slow to chide, and swift to bless. Praise him! Praise him!
Res - cues us from all our foes. Praise him! Praise him!

Praise him! Praise him! Glo - rious in his faith - ful - ness.
Praise him! Praise him! Wide - ly as his mer - cy flows.

4. An-gels, help us to a-dore him; Ye be-hold him face to face;

Sun and moon, bow down be-fore him, Dwell-ers all in time and space.

Praise him! Praise him! Praise him! Praise him! Praise with us the God of grace.

Ps. 103.   *H. F. Lyte*, 1793–1847.

24 UNIVERSITY. (C.M.)

In moderate time.

Probably by J. RANDALL, 1715–99.

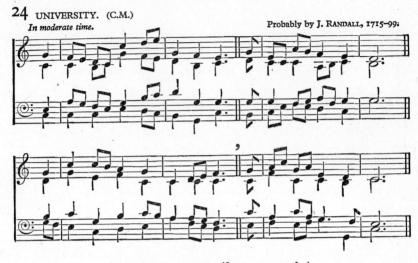

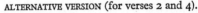

ALTERNATIVE VERSION (for verses 2 and 4).

Melody in the Tenor.

Fa-burden by MARTIN SHAW.

Ps. 23.

George Herbert, 1593–1633.

THE God of love my shepherd is,
  And he that doth me feed;
While he is mine and I am his,
  What can I want or need?

2 He leads me to the tender grass,
  Where I both feed and rest;
Then to the streams that gently pass:
  In both I have the best.

3 Or if I stray, he doth convert,
  And bring my mind in frame,
And all this not for my desert,
  But for his holy name.

4 Yea, in death's shady black abode
  Well may I walk, not fear;
For thou art with me, and thy rod
  To guide, thy staff to bear.

5 Surely thy sweet and wondrous love
  Shall measure all my days;
And, as it never shall remove,
  So neither shall my praise.

25

ST. FLAVIAN. (C.M.)

Moderately slow.

Adapted from Psalm 132 in *Day's Psalter*, 1563.

J. Keble, 1792–1866.

THERE is a book who runs may read,
    Which heavenly truth imparts,
And all the lore its scholars need,
    Pure eyes and Christian hearts.

2 The works of God, above, below,
    Within us and around,
Are pages in that book, to show
    How God himself is found.

(*Descant*) 3 The glorious sky, embracing all,
    Is like the Maker's love,
Wherewith encompassed, great and small
    In peace and order move.

4 The moon above, the Church below,
    A wondrous race they run;
But all their radiance, all their glow,
    Each borrows of its sun.

5 The raging fire, the roaring wind,
    Thy boundless power display;
But in the gentler breeze we find
    Thy Spirit's viewless way.

(*Descant*) 6 Two worlds are ours: 'tis only sin
    Forbids us to descry
The mystic heaven and earth within,
    Plain as the sea and sky.

7 Thou, who hast given me eyes to see
    And love this sight so fair,
Give me a heart to find out thee,
    And read thee everywhere.

[*For Descant see overleaf.*]

D

25 (*continued*)

Fa-burden by T. RAVENSCROFT in his *Psalter*, 1621
(rhythm slightly adapted).

MELODY.

DESCANT
AND
ACCOMPT.

J. Keble, 1792–1866.

THERE is a book who runs may read,
   Which heavenly truth imparts,
And all the lore its scholars need,
   Pure eyes and Christian hearts.

2 The works of God, above, below,
   Within us and around,
Are pages in that book, to show
   How God himself is found.

(*Descant*)
3 The glorious sky, embracing all,
   Is like the Maker's love,   [small
Wherewith encompassed, great and
   In peace and order move.

4 The moon above, the Church below,
   A wondrous race they run;
But all their radiance, all their glow,
   Each borrows of its sun.

[*For tune with melody in treble see previous page.*]

5 The raging fire, the roaring wind,
   Thy boundless power display;
   But in the gentler breeze we find
   Thy Spirit's viewless way.

(*Descant*) 6 Two worlds are ours: 'tis only sin
   Forbids us to descry
   The mystic heaven and earth within,
   Plain as the sea and sky.

7 Thou, who hast given me eyes to see
   And love this sight so fair,
   Give me a heart to find out thee,
   And read thee everywhere.

26

ST. COLUMBA. (8 7. 8 7.)
In moderate time.   Ancient Irish Hymn Melody (Original form).

Ps. 23.   *Sir H. W. Baker, 1821–77.*

THE King of love my Shepherd is,
   Whose goodness faileth never;
I nothing lack if I am his
   And he is mine for ever.

2 Where streams of living water flow
   My ransomed soul he leadeth,
And where the verdant pastures grow
   With food celestial feedeth.

3 Perverse and foolish oft I strayed,
   But yet in love he sought me,
And on his shoulder gently laid,
   And home, rejoicing, brought me.

4 In death's dark vale I fear no ill
   With thee, dear Lord, beside me;
Thy rod and staff my comfort still,
   Thy Cross before to guide me.

5 Thou spread'st a table in my sight;
   Thy unction grace bestoweth:
And O what transport of delight
   From thy pure chalice floweth!

6 And so through all the length of days
   Thy goodness faileth never;
Good Shepherd, may I sing thy praise
   Within thy house for ever.

27

MILES LANE. (C.M.)

W. SHRUBSOLE, 1760–1806.

In moderate time.

(Modern form of second line.)

crown him, crown him, crown him, crown him Lord of all.

E. Perronet, 1726–92; *and others.*

ALL hail the power of Jesus' name;
Let angels prostrate fall;
Bring forth the royal diadem
To crown him Lord of all.

2 Crown him, ye martyrs of your God,
Who from his altar call;
Praise him whose way of pain ye trod,
And crown him Lord of all.

3 Sinners, whose love can ne'er forget
The wormwood and the gall,
Go spread your trophies at his feet,
And crown him Lord of all.

4 Let every tribe and every tongue
To him their hearts enthral,
Lift high the universal song,
And crown him Lord of all.

28

HYFRYDOL. (8 7. 8 7. D.)

Slow and dignified.

Melody by R. H. PRICHARD, 1811–87.

A-men.

W. Chatterton Dix, 1837–98.

ALLELUYA, sing to Jesus,
  His the sceptre, his the throne;
Alleluya, his the triumph,
  His the victory alone:
Hark! The songs of peaceful Sion
  Thunder like a mighty flood;
Jesus, out of every nation,
  Hath redeemed us by his blood.

2 Alleluya, not as orphans
  Are we left in sorrow now;
Alleluya, he is near us,
  Faith believes, nor questions how;
Though the cloud from sight received him
  When the forty days were o'er,
Shall our hearts forget his promise,
  'I am with you evermore'?

3 Alleluya, alleluya,
  Glory be to God on high;
To the Father, and the Saviour,
  Who has gained the victory;
Glory to the Holy Spirit,
  Fount of love and sanctity;
Alleluya, alleluya,
  To the triune Majesty. Amen.

29

CHEERFUL (C.M.)
Moderately fast.

MARTIN SHAW.

Org.

[*Copyright*, 1915, *by J. Curwen & Sons, Ltd.*]

I. Watts, 1674–1748.

COME, let us join our cheerful songs
  With angels round the throne;
Ten thousand thousand are their tongues,
  But all their joys are one.

2 'Worthy the Lamb that died,' they cry,
    'To be exalted thus';
  'Worthy the Lamb,' our lips reply,
    'For he was slain for us.'

3 Jesus is worthy to receive
    Honour and power divine;
  And blessings more than we can give
    Be, Lord, for ever thine.

4 The whole creation join in one
    To bless the sacred name
  Of him that sits upon the throne,
    And to adore the Lamb.

30

CHILDHOOD. (8 8. 8 6.)
In moderate time.
'University of Wales' (*Students' Hymnal*), 1923.

Stopford A. Brooke, 1832–1916.

IT fell upon a summer day,
　When Jesus walked in Galilee,
The mothers from a village brought
　　Their children to his knee.

2 He took them in his arms, and laid
　　His hands on each remembered head;
'Suffer these little ones to come
　　To me,' he gently said.

3 'Forbid them not; unless ye bear
　　The childlike heart your hearts within,
Unto my Kingdom ye may come,
　　But may not enter in.'

4 Master, I fain would enter there;
　　O let me follow thee, and share
Thy meek and lowly heart, and be
　　Freed from all worldly care.

5 Of innocence, and love, and trust,
　　Of quiet work, and simple word,
Of joy, and thoughtlessness of self,
　　Build up my life, good Lord.

31

ABERYSTWYTH. (7 7. 7 7. D.)

Slow.

Composed or adapted by JOSEPH PARRY, 1841–1903.

[By permission of Hughes & Son, Wrexham.]

Charles Wesley, 1707–88.

JESU, lover of my soul,
  Let me to thy bosom fly,
While the nearer waters roll,
  While the tempest still is high:
Hide me, O my Saviour, hide,
  Till the storm of life is past;
Safe into the haven guide,
  O receive my soul at last.

2 Other refuge have I none;
  Hangs my helpless soul on thee;
Leave, ah! leave me not alone,
  Still support and comfort me.

(40)

All my trust on thee is stayed,
    All my help from thee I bring;
Cover my defenceless head
    With the shadow of thy wing.

3 Plenteous grace with thee is found,
    Grace to cover all my sin;
Let the healing streams abound;
    Make and keep me pure within.
Thou of life the fountain art;
    Freely let me take of thee;
Spring thou up within my heart,
    Rise to all eternity.

32

WERDE MUNTER. (7 6. 7 6. 8 8. 7 7.)

From a melody by J. Schop, d. c. 1664.

St. *Theoctistus*, c. 890. *S. P. V.*

'Ιησοῦ γλυκύτατε.

JESUS, name all names above;
    Jesus, best and dearest;
Jesus, fount of perfect love,
    Holiest, tenderest, nearest;
Thou the source of grace completest,
Thou the purest, thou the sweetest;
Thou the well of power divine,
Make me, keep me, seal me thine!

(41)

33

BULSTRODE. (7 6. 7 6.)

In moderate time.

EVELYN SHARPE.

[Copyright, 1931, by Oxford University Press.]

P. Dearmer.

O DEAR and lovely Brother,
   The Son of God alone,
When we love one another
   We are thy very own.

2 In heaven thy face is hidden,
   Too near for us to see;
And each of us is bidden
   To share that heaven with thee.

34

O GOD OF LOVE. (C.M.)

Moderately slow.

'B. R.' in *The Divine Companion*, 1722.

C. Wesley, 1707–88.

O FOR a thousand tongues to sing
   My dear Redeemer's praise,
The glories of my God and King,
   The triumphs of his grace!

2 Jesus—the name that charms our fears,
   That bids our sorrows cease;
'Tis music in the sinner's ears,
   'Tis life, and health, and peace.

3 He speaks; and, listening to his voice,
   New life the dead receive,
The mournful broken hearts rejoice,
   The humble poor believe.

4 Hear him, ye deaf; his praise, ye dumb,
   Your loosened tongues employ;
Ye blind, behold your Saviour come;
   And leap, ye lame, for joy!

5 My gracious Master and my God,
   Assist me to proclaim
And spread through all the earth abroad
   The honours of thy name.

35

IRBY. (8 7. 8 7. 7 7.)
In moderate time.

H. J. GAUNTLETT, 1805–76.

Mrs. C. F. Alexander, 1823–95.

ONCE in royal David's city
   Stood a lowly cattle shed,
Where a mother laid her baby
   In a manger for his bed;
Mary was that mother mild,
Jesus Christ her little Child.

2 He came down to earth from heaven,
   Who is God and Lord of all,
And his shelter was a stable,
   And his cradle was a stall;
With the poor, and mean, and lowly,
Lived on earth our Saviour holy.

3 And through all his wondrous childhood
   He would honour and obey,
Love, and watch the lowly maiden,
   In whose gentle arms he lay;
Christian children all must be
Mild, obedient, good as he.

4 For he is our childhood's pattern,
   Day by day like us he grew,
He was little, weak, and helpless,
   Tears and smiles like us he knew;
And he feeleth for our sadness,
And he shareth in our gladness.

5 And our eyes at last shall see him,
   Through his own redeeming love,
For that child so dear and gentle
   Is our Lord in heaven above;
And he leads his children on
To the place where he is gone.

36

GAMBLE. (6 5. 6 5. D.)
In moderate time.

Adapted by MARTIN SHAW
from a melody in *John Gamble's Collection*, 1659.

[*Copyright, 1929, by Oxford University Press.*]

(*Nativity.*)

William Canton, 1845–1926.

WHEN the herds were watching
In the midnight chill,
Came a spotless lambkin
From the heavenly hill.

2 Snow was on the mountains
And the wind was cold,
When from God's own garden
Dropped a rose of gold.

3 When 'twas bitter winter,
Homeless and forlorn
In a star-lit stable
Christ the babe was born.

4 Welcome, heavenly lambkin;
Welcome, golden rose;
Alleluya, baby
In the swaddling clothes!

37

RESONET IN LAUDIBUS. (7 8. 7 11, and refrain 10 9. 7 4. 4. 10.)
Moderately fast.

German Carol Melody, 14th cent.

1. Who with-in that sta - ble cries, Gen - tle babe that in man - ger lies?

'Tis the Lord, our heart re - plies. So fol - low him, his bid - ding do for

ev - er: To - geth - er now tri - um-phant-ly cry, Tri - um-phant-ly cry, with

one ac - cord. We will praise and glo - ri - fy The Christ, the Lord!

Ev - er, ev - er, Je - sus, bea - con for our high en - dea - vour!

A. F.

WHO within that stable cries,
  Gentle babe that in manger lies?
   'Tis the Lord, our heart replies.
  So follow him, his bidding do for
    ever:
  Together now triumphantly cry,
   Triumphantly cry, with one accord.
  We will praise and glorify
   The Christ, the Lord!
    Ever, ever,
   Jesus, beacon for our high
    endeavour!

2 Who is he, the man full-grown,
  Working on in the busy town?
   'Tis the Lord, obscure, unknown.
  So follow him, his bidding do for
    ever:

3 Healing lame and blind and dumb,
  Herald now that the Kingdom's come?
   'Tis the friend of every home.
  So follow him, his bidding do for
    ever:

PART II

4 Who is he whom crowds acclaim
  As he enters Jerusalem?
   'Tis the Lord of happy fame.
  So follow him, his bidding do for
    ever:

5 Taken in Gethsemane,
  Martyred on the forlorn cross-tree?
   He who died for you and me.
  So follow him, his bidding do for
    ever:

6 From the tomb triumphant now,
  Deathless splendour upon his brow?
   He to whom all creatures bow.
  So follow him, his bidding do for
    ever:

Conclusion, for either Part

7 Passing still to every place,
  Radiant friend of the human race!
   'Tis the Lord, the fount of grace.
  So follow him, his bidding do for ever:

(*The verses may be sung as a solo, the refrain being sung by all.*)

(45)

38

BRISTOL. (C.M.)

Moderately slow.

Melody from *Ravenscroft's Psalter*, 1621.

ALTERNATIVE VERSION

MELODY.

Fa-burden by T. RAVENSCROFT, in his Psalter.

DESCANT.

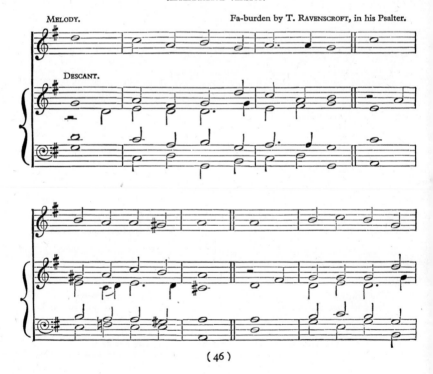

To en - rich . . the hum - ble poor.

P. Doddridge, 1702–51.

HARK the glad sound! the Saviour comes,
　The Saviour promised long!
Let every heart prepare a throne,
　And every voice a song.

2 He comes the prisoners to release
　In Satan's bondage held;
The gates of brass before him burst,
　The iron fetters yield.

(*Descant*) 3 He comes the broken heart to bind,
　The bleeding soul to cure,
And with the treasures of his grace
　To enrich the humble poor.

4 Our glad hosannas, Prince of peace,
　Thy welcome shall proclaim;
And heaven's eternal arches ring
　With thy belovèd name.

39

VENI EMMANUEL. (8 8. 8 8. 8 8.)

In free rhythm.

Adapted by T. HELMORE
'from a French Missal'.

18*th cent. Tr. T. A. Lacey.*

Veni, veni, Emmanuel.

O COME, O come, Emmanuel!
  Redeem thy captive Israel,
That into exile drear is gone
Far from the face of God's dear Son:

Rejoice! Rejoice! Emmanuel
Shall come to thee, O Israel.

2 O come, O come, thou Dayspring bright!
  Pour on our souls thy healing light;
  Dispel the long night's lingering gloom,
  And pierce the shadows of the tomb:

3 O come, thou Lord of David's key!
  The royal door fling wide and free;
  Safeguard for us the heavenward road,
  And bar the way to death's abode:

4 O come, O come, Adonäi,
  Who in thy glorious majesty
  From that high mountain clothed with awe
  Gavest thy folk the elder law;

(*For Advent see also The Spread of the Kingdom, Hymns 123–132.*)

E

40

YORKSHIRE (OR STOCKPORT). (10 10. 10 10. 10 10.)

In moderate time, dignified.

J. WAINWRIGHT, 1723–68.

John Byrom,† 1692–1763.

CHRISTIANS, awake, salute the happy morn,
Whereon the Saviour of the World was born;
Rise to adore the mystery of love,
Which hosts of angels chanted from above;
With them the joyful tidings first begun
Of God incarnate and the Virgin's Son.

2 Then to the watchful shepherds it was told,
Who heard the angelic herald's voice, 'Behold,
I bring good tidings of a saviour's birth
To you and all the nations upon earth;
This day hath God fulfilled his promised word,
This day is born a saviour, Christ the Lord.'

3 He spake; and straightway the celestial choir
　In hymns of joy, unknown before, conspire.
　The praises of redeeming love they sang,
　And heaven's whole orb with Alleluyas rang:
　God's highest glory was their anthem still,
　Peace upon earth, and unto men good will.

*4 To Bethlehem straight the enlightened shepherds ran,
　To see the wonder God had wrought for man.
　He that was born upon this joyful day
　Around us all his glory shall display:
　Saved by his love, incessant we shall sing
　Eternal praise to heaven's almighty King.

4I

WINCHESTER OLD. (C.M.)

In moderate time.　　　　　　　　　　　　First appeared in *Este's Psalter*, 1592.

Nahum Tate, 1652–1715.

WHILE shepherds watched their
　　flocks by night,
All seated on the ground,
The Angel of the Lord came down,
　And glory shone around.

2 'Fear not,' said he (for mighty dread
　Had seized their troubled mind);
'Glad tidings of great joy I bring
　To you and all mankind.

3 'To you in David's town this day
　Is born of David's line
A Saviour, who is Christ the Lord;
　And this shall be the sign:

4 'The heavenly babe you there shall find
　To human view displayed,
All meanly wrapped in swathing bands,
　And in a manger laid.'

5 Thus spake the Seraph: and forthwith
　Appeared a shining throng
Of Angels praising God, who thus
　Addressed their joyful song:

6 'All glory be to God on high,
　And to the earth be peace;
Good will henceforth from heaven to
　　men
　Begin and never cease.'

42

MENDELSSOHN. (7 7 7 7. 7 7 7 7. and refrain.)

In moderate time.　　　　Adapted from a Chorus by F. MENDELSSOHN-BARTHOLDY, 1809–47.

Organ Pedals.

[*By permission of Novello & Co., Ltd.*]

(52)

C. Wesley (1743), *G. Whitefield* (1753), *M. Madan* (1760), *and others.*

HARK! the herald angels sing
    Glory to the new-born King;
Peace on earth and mercy mild,
God and sinners reconciled:
Joyful all ye nations rise,
Join the triumph of the skies,
With the angelic host proclaim,
Christ is born in Bethlehem:

      Hark! the herald angels sing
      Glory to the new-born King.

2 Christ, by highest heaven adored,
  Christ, the everlasting Lord,
  Late in time behold him come
  Offspring of the Virgin's womb;
  Veiled in flesh the Godhead see;
  Hail the incarnate Deity!
  Pleased as man with man to dwell,
  Jesus, our Emmanuel:

3 Hail the heaven-born Prince of Peace!
  Hail the Sun of Righteousness!
  Light and life to all he brings,
  Risen with healing in his wings;
  Mild he lays his glory by,
  Born that man no more may die,
  Born to raise the sons of earth,
  Born to give them second birth:

43

ADESTE FIDELES. (Irreg.)

Slow and dignified.

18th century melody, source unknown.

Without Pedals.

Pedals.

18*th cent. Tr. F. Oakeley, and others.*

Adeste fideles.

O COME, all ye faithful,
  Joyful and triumphant,
O come ye, O come ye to Bethlehem;
Come and behold him,
Born the King of angels:
  O come, let us adore him,
  O come, let us adore him,
  O come, let us adore him, Christ the Lord!

2   See how the Shepherds,
    Summoned to his cradle,
  Leaving their flocks, draw nigh to gaze;
  We too will thither
  Bend our joyful footsteps:

HIS BIRTH

ALTERNATIVE VERSION FOR VERSES 3 AND 5

Melody in the Tenor.

Fa-burden by MARTIN SHAW.

O come, let us a - dore him, O come, let us a -
dore him, O come let us a - dore him, Christ the Lord.

[Copyright, 1924, by Martin Shaw.]

(*Descant.*)

3 Lo! star-led chieftains,
   Magi, Christ adoring,
Offer him incense, gold, and myrrh;
   We to the Christ Child
   Bring our hearts' oblations:

4 Child, for us sinners
   Poor and in the manger,
Fain we embrace thee, with love and awe;
   Who would not love thee,
   Loving us so dearly?

(*Descant.*)

5 Sing, choirs of Angels,
   Sing in exultation,
Sing, all ye citizens of heaven above;
   Glory to God
   In the highest;
      (*Christmas Day only.*)

6 Yea, Lord, we greet thee,
   Born this happy morning,
Jesu, to thee be glory given;
   Word of the Father,
   Now in flesh appearing:

(55)

44

FOREST GREEN. (D.C.M. Irreg.)

In moderate time.

English Traditional Melody.

Bishop Phillips Brooks, 1835-93.

O LITTLE town of Bethlehem,
How still we see thee lie!
Above thy deep and dreamless sleep
The silent stars go by.
Yet in thy dark streets shineth
The everlasting light;
The hopes and fears of all the years
Are met in thee to-night.

2 O morning stars, together
Proclaim the holy birth,
And praises sing to God the King,
And peace to men on earth;
For Christ is born of Mary;
And, gathered all above,
While mortals sleep, the angels keep
Their watch of wondering love.

3 How silently, how silently,
The wondrous gift is given!
So God imparts to human hearts
The blessings of his heaven.

No ear may hear his coming;
But in this world of sin,
Where meek souls will receive him, still
The dear Christ enters in.

4 Where children pure and happy
Pray to the blessèd Child,
Where misery cries out to thee,
Son of the mother mild;
Where charity stands watching
And faith holds wide the door,
The dark night wakes, the glory breaks,
And Christmas comes once more.

5 O holy Child of Bethlehem,
Descend to us, we pray;
Cast out our sin, and enter in,
Be born in us to-day.
We hear the Christmas Angels
The great glad tidings tell:
O come to us, abide with us,
Our Lord Emmanuel.

45

RODMELL. (C.M.)

In moderate time.

English Traditional Melody.

Laurence Housman.

WHEN Christ was born in Bethlehem,
Fair peace on earth to bring,
In lowly state of love he came
To be the children's King.

2 A mother's heart was there his throne,
His orb a maiden's breast,
Whereby he made through love alone
His kingdom manifest.

3 And round him, then, a holy band
Of children blest was born,
Fair guardians of his throne to stand
Attendant night and morn.

4 And unto them this grace was given
A saviour's name to own,
And die for him who out of heaven
Had found on earth a throne.

5 O blessèd babes of Bethlehem,
Who died to save our King,
Ye share the martyrs' diadem,
And in their anthem sing!

6 Your lips, on earth that never spake,
Now sound the eternal word;
And in the courts of love ye make
Your children's voices heard.

7 Lord Jesus Christ, eternal Child,
Make thou our childhood thine;
That we with thee the meek and mild
May share the love divine.

46

DIX. (7 7. 7 7. 7 7.)

In moderate time. Abridged from a Chorale, 'Treuer Heiland', by C. KOCHER, 1786-1872.

W. Chatterton Dix, 1837–98.

AS with gladness men of old
Did the guiding star behold,
As with joy they hailed its light,
Leading onward, beaming bright,
So, most gracious God, may we
Evermore be led to thee.

2 As with joyful steps they sped
To that lowly manger-bed,
There to bend the knee before
Him whom heaven and earth adore,
So may we with willing feet
Ever seek thy mercy-seat.

3 As they offered gifts most rare
At that manger rude and bare,
So may we with holy joy,
Pure, and free from sin's alloy,
All our costliest treasures bring,
Christ, to thee our heavenly King.

4 Holy Jesus, every day
Keep us in the narrow way;
And, when earthly things are past,
Bring our ransomed souls at last
Where they need no star to guide,
Where no clouds thy glory hide.

5 In the heavenly country bright
Need they no created light;
Thou its light, its joy, its crown,
Thou its sun which goes not down·
There for ever may we sing
Alleluyas to our King.

47

STUTTGART. (8 7. 8 7.)
Moderately slow, majestically.   Adapted from a melody in *Psalmodia Sacra*, Gotha, 1715.

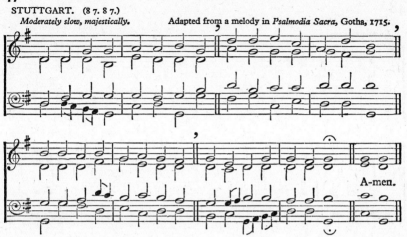

A-men.

Prudentius, b. 348.   Tr. E. Caswall.

O sola magnarum urbium.

BETHLEHEM, of noblest cities
   None can once with thee compare;
Thou alone the Lord from heaven
   Didst for us incarnate bear.

2 Fairer than the sun at morning
   Was the star that told his birth;
To the lands their God announcing,
   Hid beneath a form of earth.

3 By its lambent beauty guided
   See the eastern kings appear;
See them bend, their gifts to offer,
   Gifts of incense, gold, and myrrh.

4 Solemn things of mystic meaning:
   Incense doth the God disclose,
Gold a royal child proclaimeth,
   Myrrh a future tomb foreshows.

5 Holy Jesu, in thy brightness
   To the Gentile world displayed,
With the Father and the Spirit
   Endless praise to thee be paid.

(*For Epiphany see also The Spread of the Kingdom, Hymns 123–132.*)

(59)

48

AVE MARIA KLARE. (7 6. 7 6. 6 7 6.)
In moderate time.

Melody and harmony from
Psalteriolum Harmonicum, 1642.

Jan Struther.

WHEN Mary brought her treasure
　　Unto the holy place,
No eye of man could measure
　　The joy upon her face.
　　　He was but six weeks old,
Her plaything and her pleasure,
　　Her silver and her gold.

2 Then Simeon, on him gazing
　　With wonder and with love,
His aged voice up-raising
　　Gave thanks to God above:
　　　'Now welcome sweet release!
For I, my saviour praising,
　　May die at last in peace.'

3 And she, all sorrow scorning,
　　Rejoiced in Jesus' fame.
The child her arms adorning
　　Shone softly like a flame
　　　That burns the long night through,
And keeps from dusk till morning
　　Its vigil clear and true.

4 As by the sun in splendour
　　The flags of night are furled,
So darkness shall surrender
　　To Christ who lights the world:
　　　To Christ the star of day,
Who once was small and tender,
　　A candle's gentle ray.

49

HEINLEIN (AUS DER TIEFE). (7 7. 7 7.)

Slow.

Probably by MARTIN HERBST, 1654-81.

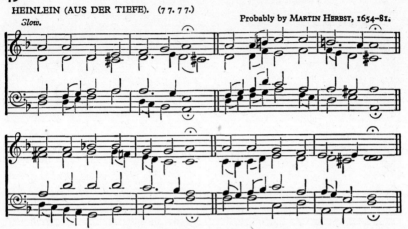

G. H. Smyttan (1856), and others.

FORTY days and forty nights
  Thou wast fasting in the wild;
Forty days and forty nights
  Tempted still, yet unbeguiled:

2 Sunbeams scorching all the day,
  Chilly dew-drops nightly shed,
Prowling beasts about thy way,
  Stones thy pillow, earth thy bed.

3 Let us thy endurance share
  And from earthly greed abstain,
With thee watching unto prayer,
  With thee strong to suffer pain.

*4 Then if evil on us press,
  Flesh or spirit to assail,
Victor in the wilderness,
  Help us not to swerve or fail!

5 So shall peace divine be ours;
  Holier gladness ours shall be;
Come to us angelic powers,
  Such as ministered to thee.

6 Keep, O keep us, Saviour dear,
  Ever constant by thy side,
That with thee we may appear
  At the eternal Eastertide.

(*For Lent hymns see also The Way of Life, 62–79, and Prayer, 112–122.*)

(*For our Lord's ministry see 30, 37, 65, 73, 77.*)

ST. THEODULPH (VALET WILL ICH DIR GEBEN). (7 6. 7 6. D.)

Melody by M. TESCHNER, *c.* 1613. Adapted and harmonized by J. S. BACH.

Palm Sunday.

St. Theodulph of Orleans, d. 821. Tr. J. M. Neale.

Gloria, laus et honor.

ALL glory, laud, and honour
    To thee, Redeemer, King,
To whom the lips of children
    Made sweet hosannas ring.

2 Thou art the King of Israel,
    Thou David's royal Son,
Who in the Lord's name comest,
    The King and blessèd one:

3 The company of angels
    Are praising thee on high,
And mortal men and all things
    Created make reply:

4 The people of the Hebrews
    With palms before thee went;
Our praise and prayer and anthems
    Before thee we present:

5 To thee before thy passion
    They sang their hymns of praise;
To thee now high exalted
    Our melody we raise:

6 Thou didst accept their praises:
    Accept the prayers we bring,
Who in all good delightest,
    Thou good and gracious King:

(62)

51

COME, FAITHFUL PEOPLE. (8 8 8. 7.)

Melody by C. BICKNELL, 1842–1918.

Moderately fast.

Palm Sunday.   *G. Moultrie* (1867) *and others.*

COME, faithful people, come away,
  Your homage to your monarch pay;
It is the feast of palms to-day:
  Hosanna in the highest!

2 When Christ, the Lord of all, drew nigh
  On Sunday morn to Bethany,
  He called two loved ones standing by:

3 'To yonder village go,' said he,
  'Where you a tethered ass shall see;
  Loose it and bring it unto me':

4 The two upon their errand sped,
  And brought the ass as he had said,
  And on its back their clothes they spread:

5 They set him on his throne so rude;
  Before him went the multitude,
  And in the way their garments strewed:

6*Go, Saviour, thus to triumph borne,
  Thy crown shall be the wreath of thorn,
  Thy royal garb the robe of scorn:

7*They thronged before, behind, around,
  They cast palm-branches on the ground,
  And still rose up the joyful sound:

8*'Blessèd is Israel's King,' they cry;
  'Blessèd is he that cometh nigh
  In name of God the Lord most high':

9 Thus, Saviour, to thy Passion go;
  Pass through the fleeting ebb and flow,
  To meet the yet unconquered foe:

NOTE.—*Certain verses may be sung by different voices: the refrain (and the first
and last verses) being sung by all.*)

(63)

52

WINCHESTER NEW. (L.M.)

Slow and dignified.   Adapted from a Chorale in the *Musikalisches Handbuch*, Hamburg, 1690.

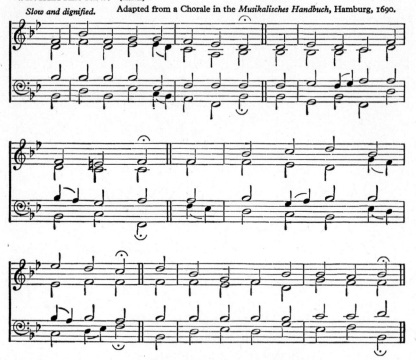

Palm Sunday.   *H. H. Milman, 1791–1868.*

RIDE on! ride on in majesty!
Hark, all the tribes hosanna cry;
Thine humble beast pursues his road
With palms and scattered garments strowed.

2 Ride on! ride on in majesty!
In lowly pomp ride on to die:
O Christ, thy triumphs now begin
O'er captive death and conquered sin.

3 Ride on! ride on in majesty!
The wingèd squadrons of the sky
Look down with sad and wondering eyes
To see the approaching sacrifice.

4 Ride on! ride on in majesty!
The last and fiercest strife is nigh;
The Father, on his sapphire throne,
Expects his own anointed Son.

5. Ride on! ride on in majesty!
In lowly pomp ride on to die;
Bow thy meek head to mortal pain,
Then take, O God, thy power, and reign.

53

HORSLEY. (C.M.)

In moderate time.　　　　　　　　　　　　　　　W. HORSLEY, 1774–1858.

ALTERNATIVE VERSION (for one or more verses).

Melody in the Tenor.　　　　　　　　　　Fa-burden by PATRICK HARVEY.

[*Copyright, 1931, by Oxford University Press.*]

Mrs. C. F. Alexander, 1823–95.

THERE is a green hill far away,
　　Without a city wall,
Where the dear Lord was crucified
　　Who died to save us all.

2 We may not know, we cannot tell,
　　What pains he had to bear,
But we believe it was for us
　　He hung and suffered there.

3 He died that we might be forgiven,
　　He died to make us good;
That we might go at last to heaven,
　　Saved by his precious blood.

4 O, dearly, dearly has he loved,
　　And we must love him too,
And trust in his redeeming blood,
　　And try his works to do.

(65)　　　　　　　　　　　　　　　　　　　　F

54

ROCKINGHAM. (L.M.)

Very slow.

Adapted by E. MILLER, 1731-1807.

I. Watts, 1674-1748.

WHEN I survey the wondrous Cross,
On which the Prince of glory died,
My richest gain I count but loss,
And pour contempt on all my pride.

2 Forbid it, Lord, that I should boast
Save in the death of Christ my God;
All the vain things that charm me most,
I sacrifice them to his blood.

3 See from his head, his hands, his feet,
Sorrow and love flow mingled down;
Did e'er such love and sorrow meet,
Or thorns compose so rich a crown?

4 Were the whole realm of nature mine,
That were a present far too small;
Love so amazing, so divine,
Demands my soul, my life, my all.

(66)

55

EASTER HYMN. (7 4. 7 4. D.)

Altered from melody in *Lyra Davidica*, 1708.

Lyra Davidica (1708), *and the Supplement* (1816).

JESUS Christ is risen to-day, *Alleluya!*
  Our triumphant holy day, *Alleluya!*
Who did once, upon the cross, *Alleluya!*
Suffer to redeem our loss. *Alleluya!*

2 Hymns of praise then let us sing
  Unto Christ, our heavenly King,
  Who endured the cross and grave,
  Sinners to redeem and save:

3 But the pains that he endured
  Our salvation have procured;
  Now above the sky he's King,
  Where the angels ever sing;

(67)

56

O FILII ET FILIAE (2). (8 8 8. and Alleluyas.)   Proper melody (modern version) as
given in Webbe's *Motetts or Antiphons*, 1792.

In moderate time.

Ascribed to 17th cent. Tr. J. M. Neale.‡

O filii et filiae.

ALLELUYA! *Alleluya! Alleluya!*
Ye sons and daughters of the King,
Whom heavenly hosts in glory sing,
To-day the grave hath lost its sting:
          Alleluya!

2 On that first morning of the week,
Before the day began to break,
The Marys went their Lord to seek:
          Alleluya!

3 A young man bade their sorrow flee,
For thus he spake unto the three:
'Your Lord is gone to Galilee':
          Alleluya!

4 That night the Apostles met in fear,
Amidst them came their Lord most
dear,
And greeted them with words of cheer:
          Alleluya!

5 When Thomas afterwards had heard
That Jesus had fulfilled his word,
He doubted if it were the Lord:
Alleluya!

6 'Thomas, behold my side,' saith he,
'My hands, my feet, my body see;
And doubt not, but believe in me':
Alleluya!

7 No longer Thomas then denied;
He saw the feet, the hands, the side;
'Thou art my Lord and God,' he cried:
Alleluya!

*8 Blessèd are they that have not seen,
And yet whose faith hath constant been,
In life eternal they shall reign:
Alleluya!

(NOTE.--*Verses 2–7 may be sung by alternate voices: the Alleluyas and first and last verses being sung by all.*)

57

VULPIUS (GELOBT SEI GOTT). (8 8 8. 4.)
In moderate time.

Melody from M. VULPIUS' *Gesangbuch* (1609).
Harmonized by HENRY G. LEY.

Al - le - lu - ya! Al - le - lu - ya! Al - le - lu - ya!

[*Copyright*, 1925, *by Oxford University Press.*]

C. A. Alington.

GOOD Christian men rejoice and sing!
Now is the triumph of our King!
To all the world glad news we bring:
Alleluya!

2 The Lord of Life is risen for ay;
Bring flowers of song to strew his way;
Let all mankind rejoice and say:

3 Praise we in songs of victory
That Love, that Life which cannot die,
And sing with hearts uplifted high:

4 Thy name we bless, O risen Lord,
And sing to-day with one accord
The life laid down, the Life restored:

58

VICTORY. (8 8. 8 4.)
Slow and dignified.

First three lines adapted from a 'Gloria Patri' by
G. P. DA PALESTRINA, 1525–94. Alleluya by W. H. MONK.

Ascribed to 18th cent. Tr. F. Pott.

Finita jam sunt praelia.

THE strife is o'er, the battle done;
Now is the Victor's triumph won;
O let the song of praise be sung:
     Alleluya!

2 Death's mightiest powers have done their worst,
And Jesus hath his foes dispersed;
Let shouts of praise and joy outburst:

3 On the third morn he rose again
Glorious in majesty to reign;
O let us swell the joyful strain:

4 Lord, by the stripes which wounded thee,
From death's dread sting thy servants free,
That we may live, and sing to thee:

(70)

59 AVE VIRGO VIRGINUM. (7 6. 7 6. D.)

Leisentritt's *Gesangbuch*, 1584 (rhythm of bar 7 slightly simplified).

In moderate time.

St. *John Damascene, c.* 750. *Pr. J. M. Neale.*‡

Ἀΐσωμεν πάντες λαοί.

COME, ye faithful, raise the strain
    Of triumphant gladness;
God hath brought his people now
    Into joy from sadness;
'Tis the spring of souls to-day;
    Christ hath burst his prison,
And from three days' sleep in death
    As a sun hath risen.

2 Now the queen of seasons, bright
    With the day of splendour,
With the royal feast of feasts,
    Comes its joy to render;
Comes to gladden Christian men,
    Who with true affection
Welcome in unwearied strains
    Jesus' resurrection.

3 Neither might the gates of death,
    Nor the tomb's dark portal,
Nor the wrappings, nor the stone,
    Hold thee as a mortal;
But to-day amidst the twelve
    Thou didst stand, bestowing
Thine own peace which evermore
    Passeth human knowing.

60

ST. MAGNUS (NOTTINGHAM). (C.M.)

Moderately slow.

Probably by J. CLARK, 1670-1707.

(Other occasions also.)

T. Kelly, 1769–1854.

THE head that once was crowned with thorns
Is crowned with glory now:
A royal diadem adorns
The mighty victor's brow.

2 The highest place that heaven affords
Is his, is his by right,
The King of kings and Lord of lords,
And heaven's eternal Light;

3 The joy of all who dwell above,
The joy of all below,
To whom he manifests his love,
And grants his name to know.

4 To them the cross, with all its shame,
With all its grace, is given:
Their name an everlasting name,
Their joy the joy of heaven.

5 They suffer with their Lord below,
They reign with him above,
Their profit and their joy to know
The mystery of his love.

6 The cross he bore is life and health,
Though shame and death to him;
His people's hope, his people's wealth,
Their everlasting theme.

61 FORTEM VIRILI PECTORE. (7 7. 7 7. D.)

In moderate time, with vigour.

German melody, Strasbourg, 1697.

(Other occasions also.)

F. C. Burkitt.

OUR Lord, his Passion ended,
Hath gloriously ascended,
Yet though from him divided,
He leaves us not unguided;
  All his benefits to crown
  He hath sent his Spirit down,
  Burning like a flame of fire
  His disciples to inspire.

2 God's Spirit is directing,
No more they sit expecting,
But forth to all the nation
They go with exultation;
  That which God in them hath wrought
  Fills their life and soul and thought,
  So their witness now can do
  Work as great in others too.

3 The centuries go gliding,
But still we have abiding
With us that Spirit holy
To make us brave and lowly—
  Lowly, for we feel our need,
  God alone is strong indeed;
  Brave, for with the Spirit's aid
  We can venture unafraid.

(Suitable also for Whitsuntide. See also hymns 80–83. For Trinity (since the Trinity is also the Unity of God), hymns 1–12 are suitable: especially 3.)

(73)

62

MELLING. (7 7. 7 7.)

With vigour.

From *A New Set of Sacred Music*
by JOHN FAWCETT, 1830.

J. Cennick, 1718–55.

CHILDREN of the heavenly King,
  As ye journey sweetly sing;
Sing your Saviour's worthy praise,
Glorious in his works and ways.

2 We are travelling home to God
In the way the fathers trod;
They are happy now, and we
Soon their happiness shall see.

3 Fear not, brethren, joyful stand
On the borders of your land;
Jesus Christ, your Father's Son,
Bids you undismayed go on.

4 Lord, obediently we go,
Gladly leaving all below;
Only thou our leader be,
And we still will follow thee.

63

DUKE STREET. (L.M.)
In moderate time.

J. HATTON, d. 1793.

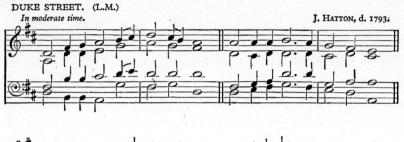

J. S. B. Monsell, 1811–75.

FIGHT the good fight with all thy might,
  Christ is thy strength, and Christ thy right;
Lay hold on life, and it shall be
Thy joy and crown eternally.

2 Run the straight race through God's good grace,
  Life up thine eyes, and seek his face;
  Life with its way before us lies,
  Christ is the path, and Christ the prize.

3 Cast care aside, upon thy Guide
  Lean, and his mercy will provide;
  Lean, and the trusting soul shall prove
  Christ is its life, and Christ its love.

4 Faint not nor fear, his arms are near,
  He changeth not, and thou art dear;
  Only believe, and thou shalt see
  That Christ is all in all to thee.

64

BINCHESTER. (C.M.)

In moderate time.

W. CROFT, 1678–1727.

Y. H., *based on* O quam juvat. C. *Coffin* (1736).

HAPPY are they, they that love God,
　Whose hearts have Christ confest,
Who by his cross have found their life,
　And 'neath his yoke their rest.

2 Glad is the praise, sweet are the songs,
　When they together sing;
And strong the prayers that bow the ear
　Of heaven's eternal King.

3 Christ to their homes giveth his peace,
　And makes their loves his own:
But ah, what tares the evil one
　Hath in his garden sown.

4 Sad were our lot, evil this earth,
　Did not its sorrows prove
The path whereby the sheep may find
　The fold of Jesus' love.

5 Then shall they know, they that love him,
　How all their pain is good;
And death itself cannot unbind
　Their happy brotherhood.

65

PLEADING SAVIOUR. (8 7. 8 7. D.)

In moderate time.

Plymouth Collection (U.S.A.), 1855.

W. *Charter Piggott.*

HEAVENLY Father, may thy blessing
  Rest upon thy children now,
When in praise thy name they hallow,
  When in prayer to thee they bow:
In the wondrous story reading
  Of the Lord of truth and grace,
May they see thy love reflected
  In the light of his dear face.

2 May they learn from this great story
  All the arts of friendliness;
Truthful speech and honest action,
  Courage, patience, steadfastness;
How to master self and temper,
  How to make their conduct fair;
When to speak and when be silent,
  When to do and when forbear.

3 May his spirit wise and holy
  With his gifts their spirits bless,
Make them loving, joyous, peaceful,
  Rich in goodness, gentleness,
Strong in self-control, and faithful,
  Kind in thought and deed; for he
Sayeth, 'What ye do for others
  Ye are doing unto me'.

66

DUNFERMLINE. (C.M.)
Moderately slow.

Scottish Psalter, 1615.

Charles Wesley, 1707–88.

HELP us to help each other, Lord,
Each other's cross to bear,
Let each his friendly aid afford
And feel his brother's care.

2 Up into thee, our living head,
Let us in all things grow,
Till thou hast made us free indeed,
And spotless here below.

3 Touched by the loadstone of thy love,
Let all our hearts agree;
And ever toward each other move,
And ever move toward thee.

67

OAKRIDGE LYNCH. (6 5. 6 5.)

Moderately slow.

MARTIN SHAW.

[*Copyright*, 1925, *by Martin Shaw.*]

Village Hymn.   *Norman Gale.*

HERE in the country's heart
   Where the grass is green,
Life is the same sweet life
   As it e'er hath been.

2 Trust in a God still lives,
   And the bell at morn
Floats with a thought of God
   O'er the rising corn.

3 God comes down in the rain,
   And the crop grows tall—
This is the country faith,
   And the best of all.

68

MONKS GATE. (11 11. 12 11.)

Brightly.

Adapted from an English Traditional Melody.

Pilgrim Song.

J. Bunyan (1684), *and others.*

HE who would valiant be
    'Gainst all disaster,
Let him in constancy
    Follow the Master.
There 's no discouragement
Shall make him once relent
His first avowed intent
    To be a pilgrim.

2 Who so beset him round
    With dismal stories,
Do but themselves confound—
    His strength the more is.
No foes shall stay his might,
Though he with giants fight:
He will make good his right
    To be a pilgrim.

3 Since, Lord, thou dost defend
    Us with thy Spirit,
We know we at the end
    Shall life inherit.
Then fancies flee away!
I'll fear not what men say,
I'll labour night and day
    To be a pilgrim.

69

KILMARNOCK. (C.M.)
In moderate time.

NEIL DOUGALL, 1776–1862.

Confidence.

J. *Addison*,‡ 1672–1719.

HOW are thy servants blest, O Lord!
　How sure is their defence!
Eternal Wisdom is their guide,
　Their help Omnipotence.

2 In foreign realms and lands remote,
　Supported by thy care,
Through burning climes they pass unhurt,
　And breathe in tainted air.

3 From all their griefs and dangers, Lord,
　Thy mercy sets them free,
While in the confidence of prayer
　Their souls take hold on thee.

4 In midst of dangers, fears, and death,
　Thy goodness we'll adore;
And praise thee for thy mercies past,
　And humbly hope for more.

5 Our life, while thou preserv'st that life,
　Thy sacrifice shall be;
And death, when death shall be our lot,
　Shall join our souls to thee.

70

CROMER. (L.M.)
In moderate time.
J. A. LLOYD, 1815–74.

Lucy Larcom, 1826–93.

I LEARNED it in the meadow path,
I learned it on the mountain stairs,
The best things any mortal hath
Are those which every mortal shares.

2 The air we breathe, the sky, the breeze,
The light without us and within,
Life with its unlocked treasuries,
God's riches are for all to win.

3 The grass is softer to my tread,
Because it rests unnumbered feet;
Sweeter to me the wild rose red,
Because she makes the whole world sweet.

4 And up the radiant peopled way
That opens into worlds unknown
It will be life's delight to say
'Heaven is not heaven for me alone'.

5 Wealth won by other's poverty—
Not such be mine! let me be blest
Only in what they share with me,
And what I share with all the rest.

71

BATTISHILL. (77.77.)
In moderate time.

Adapted from a melody by JONATHAN BATTISHILL, 1738-1801.

School-days.

W. Charter Piggott.

IN our work and in our play,
  Jesus, be thou ever near;
Guarding, guiding all the day,
  Keep us in thy presence dear.

2 Thou, who at thy mother's knee
    Learned to hearken and obey,
  Then, work done, ran happily
    With the children to their play;

3 And by Joseph's bench did stand,
    Holding his edged tools, as he
  Guiding them with skilful hand,
    Made a carpenter of thee;

4 Help us, that with eager mind
    We may learn both fact and rule,
  Patient, diligent and kind
    In the comradeship of school.

5 Help us, too, in sport and game
    Gallantly to play our part;
  Win or lose, to keep the same
    Dauntless spirit and brave heart.

6 May we grow like him in grace,
    True in mind and pure of soul,
  Meeting life with steadfast face,
    Run its race and reach the goal.

(83)

72

CAMBER. (6 5. 6 5.)

Rather slowly.

MARTIN SHAW.

[*Copyright, 1931, by Martin Shaw.*]

Mrs. J. A. Carney‡ (1845).

LITTLE drops of water,
Little grains of sand,
Make the mighty ocean
And the beauteous land.

2 Little deeds of kindness,
Little words of love,
Make our earth an Eden,
Like the heavens above.

3 Little seeds of mercy
Sown by youthful hands,
Grow to bless the nations
Far in other lands.

4 Glory then for ever
Be to God on high,
Beautiful and loving,
To eternity.

73

SLANE. (10 11. 11 12.)
In moderate time.   Irish Traditional Melody.

All-Day Hymn.   *Jan Struther.*

LORD of all hopefulness, Lord of all joy,
Whose trust, ever child-like, no cares could destroy,
Be there at our waking, and give us, we pray,
Your bliss in our hearts, Lord, at the break of the day.

2 Lord of all eagerness, Lord of all faith,
Whose strong hands were skilled at the plane and the lathe,
Be there at our labours, and give us, we pray,
Your strength in our hearts, Lord, at the noon of the day.

3 Lord of all kindliness, Lord of all grace,
Your hands swift to welcome, your arms to embrace,
Be there at our homing, and give us, we pray,
Your love in our hearts, Lord, at the eve of the day.

4 Lord of all gentleness, Lord of all calm,
Whose voice is contentment, whose presence is balm,
Be there at our sleeping, and give us, we pray,
Your peace in our hearts, Lord, at the end of the day.

74

IL BUON PASTOR. (8 7. 8 7 7.)
Moderately fast.

Adapted from a melody in *Canzuns Spirituaelas*
(Upper Engadine), 1765.

P. Dearmer.

LORD of health, thou life within us,
  Strength of all that lives and grows,
Love that meets our hearts to win us,
  Beauty that around us glows,
  Take the praise that brims and flows!

2 Praise for all our work and leisure,
    Mirth and games and jollity,
  Study, science, all the treasure
    That is stored by memory,
    Skill of mind and hand and eye;

3 Praise for joys, for sorrows even,
    All that leads us up to thee;
  Most of all that out from heaven
    Came thy Son to set us free,
    Came to show us what to be.

4 May our work be keen and willing;
    Make us true to thee and wise;
  Help us now, each moment filling,
    Skill and service be our prize,
    Till to thy far hills we rise.

75

RAVENSHAW. (6 6. 6 6.)

Moderately slow.

Melody abridged by W. H. MONK, from *Ave Hierarchia*
(M. WEISSE, 1480–1534).

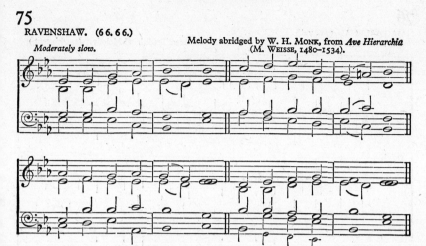

Sir H. W. Baker,† 1821–77.

LORD, thy word abideth,
   And our footsteps guideth;
Who its truth believeth
Light and joy receiveth.

2 When our foes are near us,
   Then thy word doth cheer us,
   Word of consolation,
   Message of salvation.

3 When the storms are o'er us
   And dark clouds before us,
   Then its light directeth
   And our way protecteth.

4 Who can tell the pleasure,
   Who recount the treasure,
   By thy word imparted
   To the simple-hearted?

5 Word of mercy, giving
   Succour to the living;
   Word of life, supplying
   Comfort to the dying.

6 O that we, discerning
   Its most holy learning,
   Lord, may love and hear thee,
   Evermore be near thee!

76

MAGDALENA. (7 6, 7 6.)
In moderate time.

German Traditional Melody. (*c.* 16th cent.)

Truth.

Ernest Myers, 1844–1921.

NOW in life's breezy morning
   Here on life's sunny shore,
To all the powers of falsehood
   We vow eternal war:

2 Eternal hate to falsehood;
   And then, as needs must be,
O Truth, O lady peerless,
   Eternal love to thee.

3 All fair things that seem true things,
   Our hearts shall ay receive,
Not over-quick to seize them,
   Nor over-loth to leave;

4 Not over-loth or hasty
   To leave them or to seize,
Not eager still to wander
   Nor clinging still to ease.

5 But one vow links us ever,
   That whatsoe'er shall be,
Nor life nor death shall sever
   Our souls, O Truth, from thee.

77

CHERRY TREE. (7 6. 7 6.)

In moderate time, not slow.

Traditional English Carol Melody.

J. M. Neale, 1818–66.

O HAPPY band of pilgrims,
  If onward ye will tread
With Jesus as your fellow
  To Jesus as your Head!

2 O happy if ye labour
  As Jesus did for men;
O happy if ye hunger
  As Jesus hungered then!

3 The trials that beset you,
  The sorrows ye endure,
The manifold temptations
  That death alone can cure,

4 What are they but his jewels
  Of right celestial worth?
What are they but the ladder
  Set up to heaven on earth?

5 O happy band of pilgrims,
  Look upward to the skies,
Where such a light affliction
  Shall win you such a prize!

78

UNIVERSITY COLLEGE. (7 7. 7 7.)

Moderately fast.

H. J. GAUNTLETT, 1805-76.

H. Kirke White (1806), *and others* (1812-33).

OFT in danger, oft in woe,
  Onward, Christians, onward go;
Bear the toil, maintain the strife,
Strengthened with the Bread of Life.

2 Onward, Christians, onward go,
Join the war, and face the foe;
Will ye flee in danger's hour?
Know ye not your Captain's power?

3 Let your drooping hearts be glad;
March in heavenly armour clad;
Fight, nor think the battle long:
Victory soon shall tune your song.

4 Let not sorrow dim your eye,
Soon shall every tear be dry;
Let not fears your course impede,
Great your strength, if great your need.

5 Onward then in battle move;
More than conquerors ye shall prove;
Though opposed by many a foe,
Christian soldiers, onward go.

79

MARCHING. (8 7. 8 7.)

With vigour.

MARTIN SHAW.

[*Copyright, 1915, by J. Curwen & Sons, Ltd.*]

B. S. *Ingemann*, 1789–1862.   Tr. S. *Baring-Gould*.

Igjennem Nat og Trængsel.

THROUGH the night of doubt and sorrow
　Onward goes the pilgrim band,
Singing songs of expectation,
　Marching to the Promised Land.

2 Clear before us through the darkness
　Gleams and burns the guiding light;
Brother clasps the hand of brother,
　Stepping fearless through the night.

3 One the light of God's own presence
　O'er his ransomed people shed,
Chasing far the gloom and terror,
　Brightening all the path we tread;

4 One the object of our journey,
　One the faith which never tires,
One the earnest looking forward,
　One the hope our God inspires:

5 One the strain that lips of thousands
　Lift as from the heart of one;
One the conflict, one the peril,
　One the march in God begun;

6 One the gladness of rejoicing
　On the far eternal shore,
Where the one almighty Father
　Reigns in love for evermore.

80

CARLISLE. (S.M.)
Moderately slow, dignified.

C. LOCKHART, 1745–1815.

Edwin Hatch, 1835–89.

BREATHE on me, Breath of God,
Fill me with life anew,
That I may love what thou dost love,
And do what thou wouldst do.

2 Breathe on me, Breath of God,
Until my heart is pure,
Until with thee I will one will,
To do and to endure.

3 Breathe on me, Breath of God,
Blend all my soul with thine,
Until this earthly part of me
Glows with the fire divine.

4 Breathe on me, Breath of God,
So shall I never die,
But live with thee the perfect life
Of thine eternity.

81

ST. EDMUND. (S.M.)

Moderately slow.

Adapted from Hymn Melody by E. GILDING, d. 1782.

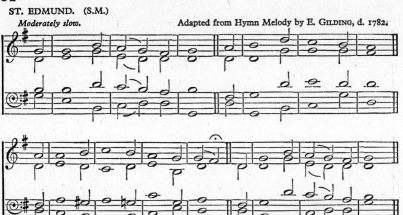

The Eternal Spirit.   *P. Dearmer.*

O HOLY Spirit, God,
    All loveliness is thine;
Great things and small are both in thee,
    The star-world is thy shrine.

2   The sunshine thou of God,
        The life of man and flower,
    The wisdom and the energy
        That fills the world with power.

3   Thou art the stream of love,
        The unity divine;
Good men and true are one in thee,
    And in thy radiance shine.

4   The heroes and the saints
        Thy messengers became;
And all the lamps that guide the world
    Were kindled at thy flame.

5   The calls that come to us
        Upon thy winds are brought;
The light that gleams beyond our dreams
    Is something thou hast thought.

6   Give fellowship, we pray,
        In love and joy and peace,
That we in counsel, knowledge, might,
    And wisdom, may increase.

82

WARRINGTON. (L.M.)
In moderate time.

R. HARRISON, 1748–1810.

A - men.

(May also be sung to MELCOMBE *(see Hymn 136) with descant, if desired, to verse 2.)*

Foundling Hospital Collection (1774).

SPIRIT of mercy, truth, and love,
Shed thy blest influence from above,
And still from age to age convey
The wonders of this sacred day.

2 In every clime, in every tongue,
Be God's eternal praises sung;
Through all the listening earth be taught
The acts our great Redeemer wrought.

3 Unfailing Comfort, heavenly Guide,
Over thy favoured Church preside;
Still may mankind thy blessings prove,
Spirit of mercy, truth, and love.

83

WOLDER (AUS MEINES HERZENS GRUNDE). (8 6. 8 6. 6 8. 8 6.)

In moderate time.

Later form of melody from WOLDER'S
Catechismus-Gesangbüchlein, 1598.

Scripture.

G. W. Briggs.

THE Spirit of the Lord revealed
  His will to saints of old,
Their heart and mind and lips unsealed
  His glory to unfold:
    In gloom of ancient night
They witnessed to the dawning word,
And in the coming of the light
    Proclaimed the coming Lord.

2 The prophets passed: at length there came,
  To sojourn and abide,
The Word incarnate, to whose name
  The prophets testified:
    The twilight overpast,
Himself the very Light of light,
As man with men, revealed at last
    The Father to our sight.

3 Eternal Spirit, who dost speak
  To mind and conscience still,
That we, in this our day, may seek
  To do our Father's will:
    Thy word of life impart,
That tells of Christ, the living Way;
Give us the quiet humble heart
    To hear and to obey.

SOLOTHURN. (L.M.)
In moderate time.

Swiss Traditional Melody.

J. M. Neale, 1818–66.

AROUND the throne of God a band
Of glorious angels always stand;
Bright things they see, sweet harps they hold,
And on their heads are crowns of gold.

2 Some wait around him, ready still
To sing his praise and do his will;
And some, when he commands them, go
To guard his servants here below.

3 Lord, give thy angels every day
Command to guide us on our way,
And bid them every evening keep
Their watch around us while we sleep.

4 So shall no wicked thing draw near,
To do us harm or cause us fear;
And we shall dwell, when life is past,
With angels round thy throne at last.

85

LAUS DEO (REDHEAD No. 46).   (8 7. 8 7.)

In moderate time.

R. REDHEAD, 1820–1901.

Bishop R. Mant, 1776–1848.

BRIGHT the vision that delighted
　Once the sight of Judah's seer;
Sweet the countless tongues united
　To entrance the prophet's ear.

2 Round the Lord in glory seated,
　Cherubim and seraphim
Filled his temple, and repeated
　Each to each the alternate hymn:

3 'Lord, thy glory fills the heaven;
　Earth is with its fullness stored;
Unto thee be glory given,
　Holy, holy, holy, Lord.'

4 Heaven is still with glory ringing,
　Earth takes up the angels' cry,
'Holy, holy, holy,' singing,
　'Lord of hosts, the Lord most high.'

H

86

RICHMOND. (C.M.)
Moderately slow.

Adapted from T. HAWEIS, 1734–1820,
by S. WEBBE (the younger).

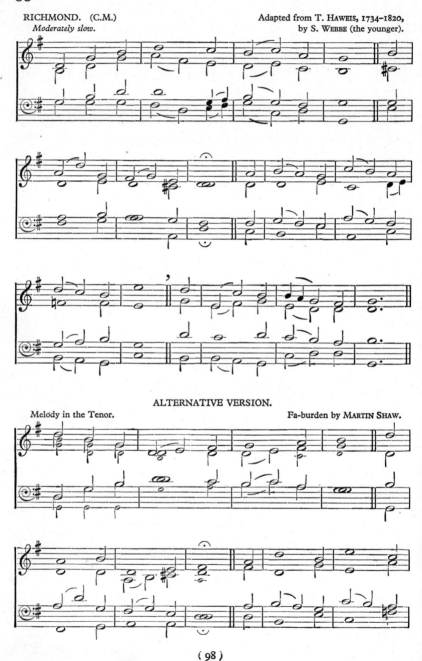

ALTERNATIVE VERSION.

Melody in the Tenor.

Fa-burden by MARTIN SHAW.

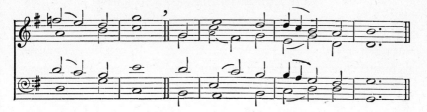

God's City.   S. *Johnson*, 1822–82.

CITY of God, how broad and far
Outspread thy walls sublime!
The true thy chartered freemen are
Of every age and clime.

(*Descant*) 2 One holy Church, one army strong,
One steadfast, high intent;
One working band, one harvest-song,
One King omnipotent.

3 How purely hath thy speech come down
From man's primeval youth!
How grandly hath thine empire grown
Of freedom, love, and truth!

(*Descant*) 4 How gleam thy watch-fires through the night
With never-fainting ray!
How rise thy towers, serene and bright,
To meet the dawning day!

5 In vain the surge's angry shock,
In vain the drifting sands:
Unharmed upon the eternal Rock
The eternal City stands.

87

SINE NOMINE. (10 10. 10. 4.)
Verses 1, 2, 3, and 7, 8.
In moderate time.

R. VAUGHAN WILLIAMS.

(small notes vv. 2, 8.)

A-men.

The Communion of Saints.   *Bishop W. W. How,* 1823–97.

FOR all the saints who from their labours rest,
Who thee by faith before the world confest,
Thy name, O Jesus, be for ever blest:
        Alleluya!

2 Thou wast their rock, their fortress, and their might;
Thou, Lord, their captain in the well-fought fight;
Thou in the darkness drear their one true light:

3 O may thy soldiers, faithful, true, and bold,
Fight as the saints who nobly fought of old,
And win, with them, the victor's crown of gold:

4*O blest communion! fellowship divine!
We feebly struggle, they in glory shine;
Yet all are one in thee, for all are thine:

5 And when the strife is fierce, the warfare long,
Steals on the ear the distant triumph-song,
And hearts are brave again, and arms are strong:

6 The golden evening brightens in the west;
Soon, soon to faithful warriors cometh rest;
Sweet is the calm of paradise the blest:

7*But lo! there breaks a yet more glorious day;
The saints triumphant rise in bright array:
The King of Glory passes on his way:

8 *From earth's wide bounds, from ocean's farthest coast,
Through gates of pearl streams in the countless host,
Singing to Father, Son, and Holy Ghost:

MEYER (ES IST KEIN TAG). (8 8. 8 4.)

Moderately slow.

Melody in J. MEYER'S *Seelenfreud*, 1692.

Commemoration.

W. Charter Piggott.

FOR those we love within the veil,
　Who once were comrades of our
　　　way,
We thank thee, Lord; for they have won
　To cloudless day;

2 And life for them is life indeed,
　The splendid goal of earth's strait
　　　race;
And where no shadows intervene
　They see thy face.

3 Not as we knew them any more,
　Toilworn, and sad with burdened
　　　care:
Erect, clear-eyed, upon their brows
　Thy name they bear.

4 Free from the fret of mortal years,
　And knowing now thy perfect will,
With quickened sense and heightened
　　　joy,
　They serve thee still.

5 O fuller, sweeter is that life,
　And larger, ampler is the air:
Eye cannot see nor heart conceive
　The glory there;

6 Nor know to what high purpose thou
　Dost yet employ their ripened powers,
Nor how at thy behest they touch
　This life of ours.

7 There are no tears within their eyes;
　With love they keep perpetual tryst;
And praise and work and rest are one
　With thee, O Christ.

89

HIGH ROAD. (10 4. 6 6. 6 6. 10 4.)
Moderately fast.

MARTIN SHAW.

[*Copyright, 1915, by J. Curwen & Sons, Ltd.*]
(*If desired, the 1st verse can be repeated after the 2nd.*)

George Herbert, 1593–1633.

LET all the world in every corner sing,
    My God and King!
The heavens are not too high,
His praise may thither fly;
The earth is not too low,
His praises there may grow.
Let all the world in every corner sing,
    My God and King!

2 Let all the world in every corner sing,
    My God and King!
The Church with psalms must shout,
No door can keep them out;
But, above all, the heart
Must bear the longest part.
Let all the world in every corner sing,
    My God and King!

90

OLD 120TH. (6 6. 6 6. 6 6.)

Moderately slow.

Melody from *Este's Psalter*, 1592.
(Rhythm slightly adapted.)

God's City.

F. T. *Palgrave*, 1824–97.

O THOU not made with hands,
   Not throned above the skies,
Nor walled with shining walls,
   Nor framed with stones of price,
More bright than gold or gem,
God's own Jerusalem!

2 Where'er the gentle heart
   Finds courage from above;
Where'er the heart forsook
   Warms with the breath of love;
Where faith bids fear depart,
City of God, thou art.

3 Thou art where'er the proud
   In humbleness melts down;
Where self itself yields up;
   Where martyrs win their crown;
Where faithful souls possess
Themselves in perfect peace;

4 Where in life's common ways
   With cheerful feet we go;
Where in his steps we tread,
   Who trod the way of woe;
Where he is in the heart,
City of God, thou art.

5 *Not throned above the skies,
   Nor golden-walled afar,
But where Christ's two or three
   In his name gathered are,
Be in the midst of them,
God's own Jerusalem!

91

RILEY. (7 7. 7 7. D.)
Brightly.

MARTIN SHAW.

[*Copyright*, 1915, *by J. Curwen & Sons, Ltd.*]

J. *Montgomery*,† 1771–1854.

SONGS of praise the angels sang,
Heaven with alleluyas rang,
When creation was begun,
When God spake and it was done.

2 Songs of praise awoke the morn
When the Prince of Peace was born:
Songs of praise arose when he
Captive led captivity.

3*Heaven and earth must pass away,
Songs of praise shall crown that day;
God will make new heavens and earth,
Songs of praise shall hail their birth.

4*And will man alone be dumb
Till that glorious kingdom come?
No, the Church delights to raise
Psalms and hymns and songs of praise.

5 Saints below, with heart and voice,
Still in songs of praise rejoice,
Learning here by faith and love
Songs of praise to sing above.

6 Hymns of glory, songs of praise,
Father, unto thee we raise;
Jesus, glory unto thee,
With the Spirit ever be.

92

MENDIP. (C.M.)

In moderate time.   English Traditional Melody.

I. *Watts*, 1674–1748.

THERE is a land of pure delight,
  Where Saints immortal reign;
Infinite day excludes the night,
  And pleasures banish pain.

2 There everlasting spring abides,
    And never-withering flowers;
  Death, like a narrow sea, divides
    This heavenly land from ours.

3 Sweet fields beyond the swelling flood
    Stand dressed in living green;
  So to the Jews old Canaan stood,
    While Jordan rolled between.

4 But timorous mortals start and shrink
    To cross this narrow sea,
  And linger shivering on the brink,
    And fear to launch away.

*5 O could we make our doubts remove,
    These gloomy doubts that rise,
  And see the Canaan that we love
    With unbeclouded eyes;

6 Could we but climb where Moses stood,
    And view the landscape o'er,
  Not Jordan's stream, nor death's cold flood,
    Should fright us from the shore!

93

ALL SAINTS. (8 7. 8 7. 7 7.)

Moderately slow, dignified.   *Darmstadt Gesangbuch,* 1698 (slightly adapted).

H. T. Schenck, 1656–1727. Tr. F. E. Cox.‡

Wer sind die vor Gottes Throne.

WHO are these, like stars appearing,
  These before God's throne who
    stand?
Each a golden crown is wearing;
  Who are all this glorious band?
    'Alleluya!' hark they sing,
    Praising loud their heavenly king.

2 Who are these of dazzling brightness,
    These in God's own truth arrayed,
  Clad in robes of purest whiteness,
    Robes whose lustre ne'er shall fade,
      Ne'er be touched by time's rude
        hand—   [band?
      Whence comes all this glorious

3 These are they who have contended
    For their Saviour's honour long,
  Wrestling on till life was ended,

Following not the sinful throng;
  These, who well the fight sustained,
  Triumph through the Lamb have
    gained.

*4 These are they whose hearts were riven,
    Sore with woe and anguish tried,
  Who in prayer full oft have striven
    With the God they glorified;
      Now, their painful conflict o'er,
      God has bid them weep no more.

*5 These like priests have watched and
      waited,
    Offering up to Christ their will,
  Soul and body consecrated,
    Day and night to serve him still:
      Now, in God's most holy place
      Blest they stand before his face.

94

DARWALL'S 148TH. (6 6. 6 6. 8 8.)
In moderate time.

J. DARWALL, 1731–89.

R. *Baxter* (1681), *and others.*

Y E holy angels bright,
  Who wait at God's right hand,
Or through the realms of light
  Fly at your Lord's command,
    Assist our song,
    For else the theme
    Too high doth seem
  For mortal tongue.

2 Ye blessèd souls at rest,
  Who ran this earthly race,
And now, from care released,
  Behold the Saviour's face,
    God's praises sound,
    As in his sight
    With sweet delight
  Ye do abound.

3 Ye saints, who toil below,
  Adore your heavenly King,
And onward as ye go
  Some joyful anthem sing;
    Take what he gives
    And praise him still,
    Through good or ill,
  Who ever lives.

4 My soul, bear thou thy part,
  Triumph in God above:
And with a well-tuned heart
  Sing thou the songs of love!
    Let all thy days
    Till life shall end,
    Whate'er he send,
  Be filled with praise.

THANKSGIVING

NATURE: THE HANDIWORK OF GOD

Spring

95

SPRINGTIME. (8 3. 8 3. 7 7. 8 7.)

In moderate time. G. W. BRIGGS.

[*Copyright,* 1929, *by Oxford University Press.*]

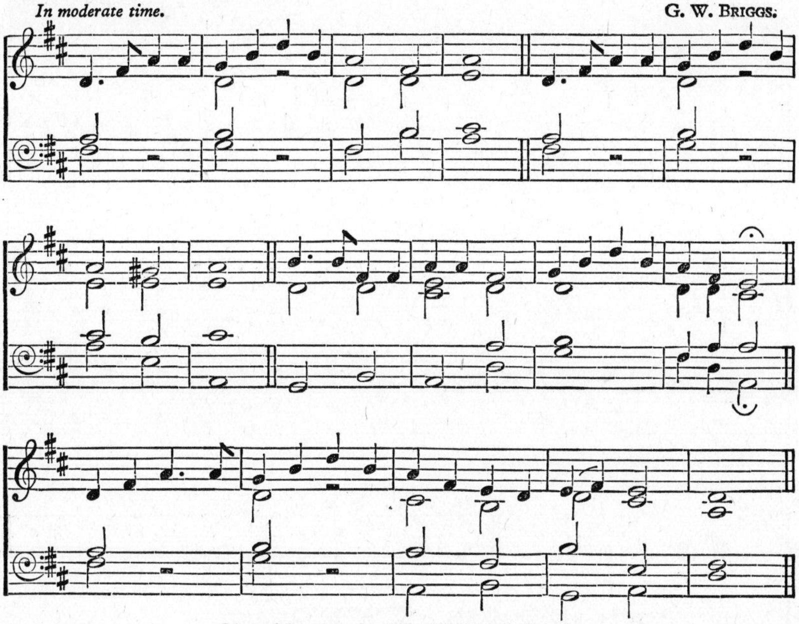

G. W. Briggs.

HARK! a hundred notes are swelling
Loud and clear.
'Tis the happy birds are telling
Spring is here!
Nature, decked in brave array,
Casts her winter robes away;
All earth's little folk rejoicing
Haste to greet the glad new day.

2 Lord and life of all things living,
Come to me:
Thou delightest but in giving;
Give to me:
Spring of joyous life thou art:
Thine own joy to me impart:
Let my praises be the outburst
Of the springtime in my heart.

96

COLOGNE (CHRISTUS IST AUFERSTANDEN). (7 7. 7 7. 14 10.)

Not too slow.   Melody from *Cölner Gesangbuch*, 1623.

Org.

Jan Struther.

SING, all ye Christian people!
  Swing, bells, in every steeple!
    For Christ to life is risen,
    Set free from death's dark prison.
With joyfulness, with joyfulness your alleluyas sing,
For Christ has come again to greet the spring.

2 Green now is on the larches;
  Springtime in triumph marches,
    And every day uncloses
    A host of new primroses:
Then daffodils and marybuds let us in garlands bring,
For Christ has come again to greet the spring.

3 Skylarks, the earth forsaking,
  Soar to their music-making,
    And in the roof-tree's hollow
    Now builds the trusting swallow:
So cries to him, so flies to him my soul on fearless wing,
For Christ has come again to greet the spring.

97 NOUS ALLONS. (65. 65. D.)

Moderately fast.

French Carol Melody.

Bishop Walsham How, 1823–97.

SUMMER suns are glowing
   Over land and sea,
Happy light is flowing
   Bountiful and free.
Everything rejoices
   In the mellow rays,
All earth's thousand voices
   Swell the psalm of praise.

2 God's free mercy streameth
   Over all the world,
And his banner gleameth
   Everywhere unfurled.
Broad and deep and glorious
   As the heaven above,
Shines in might victorious
   His eternal love.

3 Lord, upon our blindness
   Thy pure radiance pour;
For thy loving-kindness
   Make us love thee more.
And when clouds are drifting
   Dark across our sky,
Then, the veil uplifting,
   Father, be thou nigh.

4 We will never doubt thee,
   Though thou veil thy light:
Life is dark without thee;
   Death with thee is bright.
Light of light! Shine o'er us
   On our pilgrim way,
Go thou still before us
   To the endless day.

Harvest

98

ST. GEORGE. (77. 77. D.)

G. J. ELVEY, 1816–93.

Brightly.

H. Alford,‡ 1810–71.

COME, ye thankful people, come,
Raise the song of harvest-home!
All be safely gathered in,
Ere the winter storms begin;
God, our Maker, doth provide
For our wants to be supplied;
Come to God's own temple, come;
Raise the song of harvest-home!

2 All this world is God's own field,
Fruit unto his praise to yield;
Wheat and tares together sown,
Unto joy or sorrow grown;
First the blade and then the ear,
Then the full corn shall appear;
Lord of harvest, grant that we
Wholesome grain and pure may be.

3 For the Lord our God shall come,
And shall take his harvest home;
From his field shall purge away
All that doth offend to-day;
Give his angels charge at last
In the fire the tares to cast,
But the fruitful wheat to store
In his barn for evermore.

(112)

*4 Then, thou Church triumphant, come,
Raise the song of harvest-home;
All be safely gathered in,
Free from sorrow, free from sin,
There for ever purified
In God's garner to abide:
Come, ten thousand angels, come,
Raise the glorious harvest-home!

Harvest

99

MONKLAND. (7 7. 7 7.)
In moderate time.

Melody from *Hymn Tunes of the United Brethren*, 1824.
Arranged by J. WILKES (1861).

(Other occasions also.)
Ps. 136.

J. Milton,‡ 1608–74.

LET us, with a gladsome mind,
Praise the Lord, for he is kind:
  For his mercies ay endure,
  Ever faithful, ever sure.

2 Let us blaze his name abroad,
For of gods he is the God:

3 He with all-commanding might
Filled the new-made world with light:

*4 He the golden-tressèd sun
Caused all day his course to run:

*5 The hornèd moon to shine by night,
'Mid her spangled sisters bright:

6 All things living he doth feed,
His full hand supplies their need:

7 Let us, with a gladsome mind,
Praise the Lord, for he is kind:

(113)

I

100

WIR PFLÜGEN. (7 6. 7 6. 7 6. 7 6. 6 6. 8 4.)
In moderate time.

Bible Class Magazine, 1854, said to be
arranged from J. A. P. SCHULZ, 1747–1800.

NATURE: THE HANDIWORK OF GOD

M. Claudius, 1740–1815. Tr. J. M. Campbell.

WE plough the fields, and scatter
　The good seed on the land,
But it is fed and watered
　By God's almighty hand:
He sends the snow in winter,
　The warmth to swell the grain,
The breezes and the sunshine,
　And soft refreshing rain:

　　All good gifts around us
　　　Are sent from heaven above;
　　Then thank the Lord, O thank the Lord,
　　　For all his love.

2 He only is the Maker
　Of all things near and far,
He paints the wayside flower,
　He lights the evening star.
The winds and waves obey him,
　By him the birds are fed;
Much more to us, his children,
　He gives our daily bread:

3 We thank thee then, O Father,
　For all things bright and good;
The seed-time and the harvest,
　Our life, our health, our food.
No gifts have we to offer
　For all thy love imparts,
But that which thou desirest,
　Our humble, thankful hearts:

　　All good gifts around us
　　　Are sent from heaven above;
　　Then thank the Lord, O thank the Lord,
　　　For all his love.

IOI

GLENFINLAS. (6 5. 6 5.)

In moderate time.

K. G. FINLAY.

Treasure.   *Jan Struther.*

DAISIES are our silver,
 Buttercups our gold:
This is all the treasure
 We can have or hold.

2 Raindrops are our diamonds
 And the morning dew;
While for shining sapphires
 We've the speedwell blue.

3 These shall be our emeralds—
 Leaves so new and green;
Roses make the reddest
 Rubies ever seen.

4 God, who gave these treasures
 To your children small,
Teach us how to love them
 And grow like them all.

5 Make us bright as silver:
 Make us good as gold;
Warm as summer roses
 Let our hearts unfold.

6 Gay as leaves in April,
 Clear as drops of dew—
God, who made the speedwell,
 Keep us true to you.

102

ENGLAND'S LANE. (7 7. 7 7. 7 7.)
Moderately fast.

Adapted by GEOFFREY SHAW
from an English Melody.

F. S. Pierpoint,† 1835–1917.

F^{OR} the beauty of the earth,
    For the beauty of the skies,
For the love which from our birth
Over and around us lies:
    Father, unto thee we raise
    This our sacrifice of praise.

2 For the beauty of each hour
    Of the day and of the night,
Hill and vale, and tree and flower,
    Sun and moon and stars of light:

3 For the joy of ear and eye,
    For the heart and brain's delight,
For the mystic harmony
    Linking sense to sound and sight:

4 For the joy of human love,
    Brother, sister, parent, child,
Friends on earth, and friends above,
    For all gentle thoughts and mild:

5 For each perfect gift of thine
    To our race so freely given,
Graces human and divine,
    Flowers of earth and buds of heaven:

103

WATER-END. (6 5. 6 5. Irreg.)

Brightly.

GEOFFREY SHAW.

1. Glad that I live am I, That the sky is blue;

Glad for the coun - try lanes And the fall of dew.

simile.

2. Af - ter the sun the rain, Af - ter the rain the sun;

This is the way of life, Till the work be done.

3. All that we need to do, Be we low or high, Is to

see that we grow Near-er .... the sky.

Lizette Woodworth Reese.

104 NEW SABBATH. (L.M.)

In moderate time.

H. PHILLIPS, c. 1806.

Bishop G. E. L. Cotton, 1813-66.

WE thank thee, Lord, for this fair earth,
The glittering sky, the silver sea;
For all their beauty, all their worth,
Their light and glory, come from thee.

2 Thanks for the flowers that clothe the ground,
The trees that wave their arms above,
The hills that gird our dwellings round,
As thou dost gird thine own with love.

3 Yet teach us still how far more fair,
More glorious, Father, in thy sight,
Is one pure deed, one holy prayer,
One heart that owns thy Spirit's might.

4 So, while we gaze with thoughtful eye
On all the gifts thy love has given,
Help us in thee to live and die,
By thee to rise from earth to heaven.

105

ABENDLIED (DER TAG MIT SEINEM LICHTE). (7 7. 7 7 6. D.)

In moderate time.

J. G. EBELING, 1637–76.

Jan Struther.

WE thank you, Lord of Heaven,
  For all the joys that greet us,
For all that you have given
  To help us and delight us
    In earth and sky and seas;
The sunlight on the meadows,
  The rainbow's fleeting wonder,
The clouds with cooling shadows,
  The stars that shine in splendour—
    We thank you, Lord, for these.

2 For swift and gallant horses,
    For lambs in pastures springing,
  For dogs with friendly faces,
    For birds with music thronging
      Their chantries in the trees;

For herbs to cool our fever,
  For flowers of field and garden,
For bees among the clover
  With stolen sweetness laden—
    We thank you, Lord, for these.

3 For homely dwelling-places
    Where childhood's visions linger,
  For friends and kindly voices,
    For bread to stay our hunger
      And sleep to bring us ease;
  For zeal and zest of living,
    For faith and understanding,
  For words to tell our loving,
    For hope of peace unending—
      We thank you, Lord, for these.

106

SUO-GÂN. (6 6. 6 6.)
Rather slowly. v. I.

Welsh Traditional Melody.

Verse 2. *(A little quicker.)*

S. P.

WINTER creeps,
Nature sleeps;
Birds are gone,
Flowers are none,
Fields are bare,
Bleak the air,
Leaves are shed:
All seems dead.

2. God's alive!
Grow and thrive.
Hidden away,
Bloom of May,
Robe of June!
Very soon
Nought but green
Will be seen!

(*For Nature Hymns see also* 14–17, 19, 20, 25.)

107

GWALCHMAI. (7 4. 7 4. D.)
In moderate time.

J. D. JONES, 1827–70.

Praise.

George Herbert, 1593–1633.

KING of glory, King of peace,
　　I will love thee;
And that love may never cease,
　　I will move thee.
Thou hast granted my request,
　　Thou hast heard me;
Thou didst note my working breast,
　　Thou hast spared me.

2 Wherefore with my utmost art
　　I will sing thee,
And the cream of all my heart
　　I will bring thee.
Though my sins against me cried,
　　Thou didst clear me;
And alone, when they replied,
　　Thou didst hear me.

3 Seven whole days, not one in seven,
　　I will praise thee;
In my heart, though not in heaven,
　　I can raise thee.
Small it is, in this poor sort
　　To enrol thee:
E'en eternity 's too short
　　To extol thee.

108

MANOR STREET. (10 6. D.)

Rather fast,

MARTIN SHAW.

Praise him, praise him, all his chil - dren praise him! He is love, he is love. 2. Thank him, thank him, all his chil-dren thank him! He is love, he is love.

Praise.

S. P. V.

PRAISE him, praise him, all his children praise him!
He is love, he is love.

2 Thank him, thank him, all his children thank him!
He is love, he is love.

3 Love him, love him, all his children love him!
He is love, he is love.

4 Crown him, crown him, all his children crown him!
He is love, he is love.

(124)

109

WAREHAM. (L.M.)

Slow and dignified.

Later version of melody by W. KNAPP, 1698-1768.

Y. H.

REJOICE, O land, in God thy might,
His will obey, him serve aright;
For thee the Saints uplift their voice:
Fear not, O land, in God rejoice.

2 Glad shalt thou be, with blessing
crowned,
With joy and peace thou shalt abound;

Yea, love with thee shall make his
home
Until thou see God's kingdom come.

3 He shall forgive thy sins untold:
Remember thou his love of old;
Walk in his way, his word adore,
And keep his truth for evermore.

110 WAREHAM. (L.M.)

Ps. 117.

I. Watts (1719).

FROM all that dwell below the skies
Let the Creator's praise arise:
Let the Redeemer's name be sung
Through every land by every tongue.

2 Eternal are thy mercies, Lord,
Eternal truth attends thy word:
Thy praise shall sound from shore to shore,
Till suns shall rise and set no more.

III

GOPSAL. (6 6. 6 6. 8 8.)
In moderate time.

G. F. HANDEL, 1685–1759.

C. Wesley, 1707–88.

REJOICE! The Lord is King,
    Your Lord and King adore;
Mortals, give thanks and sing,
    And triumph evermore:

> *Lift up your heart, lift up your voice;*
> *Rejoice, again I say, rejoice.*

2 Jesus, the Saviour, reigns,
    The God of truth and love;
When he had purged our stains,
    He took his seat above:

3 His kingdom cannot fail;
    He rules o'er earth and heaven;
The keys of death and hell
    Are to our Jesus given:

4 He sits at God's right hand
    Till all his foes submit,
And bow to his command,
    And fall beneath his feet:

112

GOTT WILL'S MACHEN. (8 7. 8 7.)

In moderate time.

J. L. STEINER, 1688–1761.

Mrs. L. M. Willis (1864), *and others.*

FATHER, hear the prayer we offer:
    Not for ease that prayer shall be,
But for strength that we may ever
    Live our lives courageously.

2 Not for ever in green pastures
    Do we ask our way to be;
But the steep and rugged pathway
    May we tread rejoicingly.

3 Not for ever by still waters
    Would we idly rest and stay;
But would smite the living fountains
    From the rocks along our way.

4 Be our strength in hours of weakness,
    In our wanderings be our guide;
Through endeavour, failure, danger,
    Father, be thou at our side.

113

WHITE GATES. (8 8. 8 3.)

In moderate time.

R. VAUGHAN WILLIAMS.

[*Copyright,* 1931, *by R. Vaughan Williams.*]

G. Thring, 1823–1903.

FIERCE raged the tempest o'er the deep,
Watch did thine anxious servants keep,
But thou wast wrapped in guileless sleep,
Calm and still.

2 'Save, Lord, we perish!' was their cry,
'O save us in our agony!'
Thy word above the storm rose high,
'Peace, be still.'

3 The wild winds hushed; the angry deep
Sank, like a little child, to sleep;
The sullen billows ceased to leap,
At thy will.

4 So, when our life is clouded o'er,
And storm-winds drift us from the shore,
Say, lest we sink to rise no more,
'Peace, be still.'

114

QUEM PASTORES LAUDAVERE. (8 8 8. 7.)

In moderate time.

Melody from a 14th-century German MS.

P. Dearmer.

JESUS, good above all other,
  Gentle child of gentle mother,
In a stable born our brother,
      Give us grace to persevere.

2 Jesus, cradled in a manger,
  For us facing every danger,
  Living as a homeless stranger,
      Make we thee our King most dear.

3 Jesus, for thy people dying,
  Risen Master, death defying,
  Lord in heaven, thy grace supplying,
      Keep us to thy presence near.

4 Jesus, who our sorrows bearest,
  All our thoughts and hopes thou sharest,
  Thou to man the truth declarest;
      Help us all thy truth to hear.

5 Lord, in all our doings guide us;
  Pride and hate shall ne'er divide us;
  We'll go on with thee beside us,
      And with joy we'll persevere!

K

115

PEACEFIELD. (7 7. 7 7.)

Slow. Ancient Irish Lullaby, harmonized by DAVID F. R. WILSON.

Unity. *Charles Wesley*, 1707–88.

JESUS, Lord, we look to thee;
Let us in thy name agree;
Show thyself the Prince of Peace;
Bid our strife for ever cease.

2 Make us of one heart and mind,
Courteous, pitiful, and kind,
Lowly, meek, in thought and word,
Altogether like our Lord.

3 Let us each for other care,
Each the other's burden bear;
To thy Church the pattern give,
Show how true believers live.

4 Free from anger and from pride,
Let us thus in God abide;
All the depths of love express,
All the height of holiness.

116

SIMEON. (L.M.)
Moderately slow.

S. STANLEY, 1767-1822.

W. Cowper, 1731-1800.

JESUS, where'er thy people meet,
    There they behold thy mercy-seat;
Where'er they seek thee, thou art found,
And every place is hallowed ground.

2 For thou, within no walls confined,
    Inhabitest the humble mind;
Such ever bring thee where they come,
And, going, take thee to their home.

3 Dear shepherd of thy chosen few,
    Thy former mercies here renew;
Here to our waiting hearts proclaim
The sweetness of thy saving name.

4 Here may we prove the power of prayer,
    To strengthen faith and sweeten care;
To teach our faint desires to rise,
And bring all heaven before our eyes.

5 Lord, we are few, but thou art near;
    Nor short thine arm, nor deaf thine ear;
O rend the heavens, come quickly down,
And make a thousand hearts thine own!

117

ABERDEEN. (C.M.)

In moderate time.

Melody in BREMNER'S *Collection*, 1763.

J. R. Wreford, 1800–81.

LORD, while for all mankind we pray
  Of every clime and coast,
O hear us for our native land,
  The land we love the most.

2 O guard our shores from every foe;
    With peace our borders bless;
  With prosperous times our cities crown,
    Our fields with plenteousness.

3 Unite us in the sacred love
    Of knowledge, truth, and thee;
  And let our hills and valleys shout
    The songs of liberty.

4 Lord of the nations, thus to thee
    Our country we commend;
  Be thou her refuge and her trust,
    Her everlasting friend.

118

STOCKTON. (C.M.)

In moderate time.

T. WRIGHT, 1763–1829.

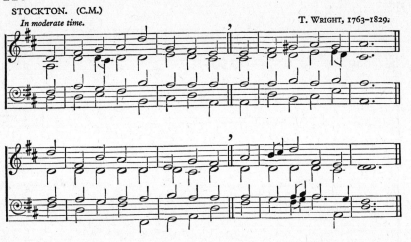

C. *Wesley*, 1707–88.

O FOR a heart to praise my God,
   A heart from sin set free:
A heart that always feels thy blood
   So freely spilt for me:

2 A heart resigned, submissive, meek,
   My dear Redeemer's throne;
Where only Christ is heard to speak,
   Where Jesus reigns alone:

3 A humble, lowly, contrite heart,
   Believing, true, and clean,
Which neither life nor death can part
   From him that dwells within:

4 A heart in every thought renewed,
   And full of love divine;
Perfect, and right, and pure, and good,
   A copy, Lord, of thine.

5 Thy nature, gracious Lord, impart,
   Come quickly from above;
Write thy new name upon my heart,
   Thy new best name of Love.

119

YORK. (C.M.)

Moderately slow.

Melody from *Scottish Psalter*, 1615.
Harmony from J. MILTON, d. 1647.

Pss. 122, 133, 116.

Scottish Psalter (1650).

PRAY that Jerusalem may have
  Peace and felicity:
Let them that love thee and thy peace
  Have still prosperity.

2 Behold how good a thing it is,
    And how becoming well,
  Together such as brethren are
    In unity to dwell.

3 Therefore I wish that peace may still
    Within thy walls remain,
  And ever may thy palaces
    Prosperity retain.

4 Now, for my friends' and brethren's sake,
    Peace be in thee, I'll say;
  And for the house of God our Lord
    I'll seek thy good alway.

119 (*cont.*)   ALTERNATIVE VERSION (for verses 2 and 4).

MELODY.   Fa-burden by S. STUBBS in *Ravenscroft's Psalter*, 1621.

Pss. 122, 133, 116.   *Scottish Psalter* (1650).

PRAY that Jerusalem may have
  Peace and felicity:
Let them that love thee and thy peace
  Have still prosperity.

(*Descant*) 2 Behold how good a thing it is,
  And how becoming well,
Together such as brethren are
  In unity to dwell.

3 Therefore I wish that peace may still
  Within thy walls remain,
And ever may thy palaces
  Prosperity retain.

(*Descant*) 4 Now, for my friends' and brethren's sake,
  Peace be in thee, I'll say;
And for the house of God our Lord
  I'll seek thy good alway.

120

MEIRIONYDD. (7 6. 7 6. D.)

In moderate time.

Later form of melody by
W. LLOYD, 1785–1852.

Mrs. J. C. Simpson (1831), and others.

PRAY when the morn is breaking,
  Pray when the noon is bright,
Pray with the eve's declining,
  Pray in the hush of night:
With mind made clear of tumult,
  All meaner thoughts away,
Make thou thy soul transparent,
  Seek thou with God to pray.

2 Remember all who love thee,
    All who are loved by thee,
  And next for those that hate thee
    Pray thou, if such there be:
  Last for thyself in meekness
    A blessing humbly claim,
  And link with each petition
    Thy great Redeemer's name.

3 But if 'tis e'er denied thee
    In solitude to pray,
  Should holy thoughts come o'er thee
    Upon life's crowded way,
  E'en then the silent breathing
    That lifts thy soul above
  Shall reach the thronèd Presence
    Of mercy, truth, and love.

121

WIGTOWN. (C.M.)
Moderately slow.

Scottish Psalter, 1635.

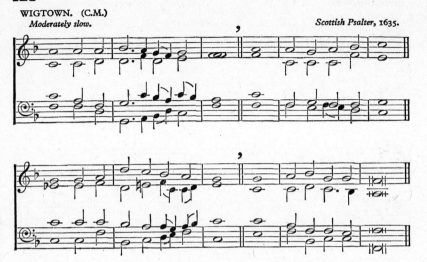

Prayer.

J. Montgomery, 1771–1854.

PRAYER is the soul's sincere desire,
  Uttered or unexpressed;
The motion of a hidden fire
  That trembles in the breast.

2 Prayer is the burden of a sigh,
    The falling of a tear,
  The upward glancing of an eye
    When none but God is near.

3 Prayer is the simplest form of speech
    That infant lips can try;
  Prayer the sublimest strains that reach
    The Majesty on high.

4 Prayer is the contrite sinner's voice,
    Returning from his ways,
  While angels in their songs rejoice,
    And cry, 'Behold, he prays!'

5 Prayer is the Christian's vital breath,
    The Christian's native air,
  His watchword at the gates of death:
    He enters heaven with prayer.

6 O thou by whom we come to God,
    The Life, the Truth, the Way,
  The path of prayer thyself hast trod:
    Lord, teach us how to pray.

122

BOYCE. (7 7. 7 7.)
In moderate time.

W. BOYCE, 1710-79.

Jane E. Leeson, 1807-82.

SAVIOUR, teach me, day by day,
  Love's sweet lesson to obey;
Sweeter lesson cannot be,
Loving him who first loved me.

2 With a child's glad heart of love
  At thy bidding may I move,
  Prompt to serve and follow thee,
  Loving him who first loved me.

3 Teach me thus thy steps to trace,
  Strong to follow in thy grace,
  Learning how to love from thee,
  Loving him who so loved me.

4 Love in loving finds employ,
  In obedience all her joy;
  Ever new that joy will be,
  Loving him who first loved me.

123

SELNECKER (NUN LASST UNS GOTT DEM HERREN). (7 7. 7 7.)

In moderate time.   Later form of melody in SELNECKER's *Christliche Psalmen*, 1587.

E. H.

A BRIGHTER dawn is breaking,
  And earth with praise is waking;
For thou, O King most highest,
The power of death defiest;

2 And thou hast come victorious,
  With risen body glorious,
Who now for ever livest,
And life abundant givest.

3 O free the world from blindness,
  And fill the world with kindness,
Give sinners resurrection,
Bring striving to perfection;

4 In sickness give us healing,
  In doubt thy clear revealing,
That praise to thee be given
In earth as in thy heaven.

124

WOODLANDS. (10 10. 10 10.)

In moderate time.

W. GREATOREX.

THE SPREAD OF THE KINGDOM

Basil Mathews.

FAR round the world thy children sing their song;
From East and West their voices sweetly blend,
Praising the Lord in whom young lives are strong,
  Jesus our guide, our hero, and our friend.

*2 Guide of the pilgrim clambering to the height,
  Hero on whom our fearful hearts depend,
Friend of the wanderer yearning for the light,
  Jesus our guide, our hero, and our friend.

3 Where thy wide ocean, wave on rolling wave,
  Beats through the ages on each island shore,
They praise their Lord, whose hand alone can save,
  Whose sea of love surrounds them evermore.

4 Thy sun-kissed children on earth's spreading plain,
  Where Asia's rivers water all the land,
Sing, as they watch thy fields of glowing grain,
  Praise to the Lord who feeds them with his hand.

5 Still there are lands where none have seen thy face,
  Children whose hearts have never shared thy joy:
Yet thou would'st pour on these thy radiant grace,
  Give thy glad strength to every girl and boy.

*6 All round the world let children sing thy song,
  From East and West their voices sweetly blend;
Praising the Lord in whom young lives are strong,
  Jesus our guide, our hero, and our friend.

125

LAUS TIBI CHRISTE. (6 5. 6 5. D.)

Moderately slow, dignified.   From a 14th-century German Processional Melody.

G. Thring, 1823–1903.

FROM the eastern mountains
  Pressing on they come,
Wise men in their wisdom,
  To his humble home;
Stirred by deep devotion,
  Hasting from afar,
Ever journeying onward,
  Guided by a star.

2 There their Lord and Saviour
    Meek and lowly lay,
  Wondrous light that led them
    Onward on their way,
  Ever now to lighten
    Nations from afar,
  As they journey homeward
    By that guiding star.

3 Thou who in a manger
    Once hast lowly lain,
  Who dost now in glory
    O'er all kingdoms reign,
  Gather in the heathen,
    Who in lands afar
  Ne'er have seen the brightness
    Of thy guiding star.

4 Gather in the outcasts,
    All who've gone astray;
  Throw thy radiance o'er them,
    Guide them on their way;
  Those who never knew thee,
    Those who've wandered far,
  Guide them by the brightness
    Of thy guiding star.

5*Onward through the darkness
    Of the lonely night,
  Shining still before them
    With thy kindly light,
  Guide them, Jew and Gentile,
    Homeward from afar,
  Young and old together,
    By thy guiding star.

6 *Until every nation,
    Whether bond or free,
  'Neath thy star-lit banner,
    Jesus, follows thee,
  O'er the distant mountains
    To that heavenly home
  Where nor sin nor sorrow
    Evermore shall come.

126

LITTLE CORNARD. (6 6. 6 6. 8 8.)

With vigour.

MARTIN SHAW.

[*Copyright*, 1915, *by J. Curwen & Sons, Ltd.*]

Charles E. Oakley, 1832–65.

1 HILLS of the North, rejoice;
    River and mountain-spring,
  Hark to the advent voice;
    Valley and lowland, sing;
  Though absent long, your Lord is nigh;
  He judgment brings and victory.

2 Isles of the southern seas,
    Deep in your coral caves
  Pent be each warring breeze,
    Lulled be your restless waves:
  He comes to reign with boundless sway,
  And makes your wastes his great high-
    way.

3 Lands of the East, awake,
    Soon shall your sons be free;
  The sleep of ages break,
    And rise to liberty.
  On your far hills, long cold and grey,
  Has dawned the everlasting day.

4 Shores of the utmost West,
    Ye that have waited long,
  Unvisited, unblest,
    Break forth to swelling song;
  High raise the note, that Jesus died,
  Yet lives and reigns, the Crucified.

5 * Shout, while ye journey home;
    Songs be in every mouth;
  Lo, from the North we come,
    From East, and West, and South.
  City of God, the bond are free,
  We come to live and reign in thee!

(144)

127

TRURO. (L.M.)
In moderate time.   *Psalmodia Evangelica,* 1790.

ALTERNATIVE VERSION (for one or more verses).

Melody in the Tenor.   Fa-burden by GEOFFREY SHAW.

I. Watts, 1674–1748.

JESUS shall reign where'er the sun
    Does his successive journeys run;
His kingdom stretch from shore to shore
Till moons shall wax and wane no more.

2 People and realms of every tongue
    Dwell on his love with sweetest song,
And infant voices shall proclaim
Their early blessings on his name.

3 Blessings abound where'er he reigns;
    The prisoner leaps to lose his chains;
The weary find eternal rest,
And all the sons of want are blest.

4 Let every creature rise and bring
    Peculiar honours to our King;
Angels descend with songs again,
And earth repeat the long amen.

L

128

PRINCE RUPERT. (6 5. 6 5. Ter.)

With vigour.

GUSTAV HOLST, from an old English March.

THE SPREAD OF THE KINGDOM

The following alternative accompaniment for the refrain may be used for one or more verses:
but only when the tune is well established.

ORGAN.

con 8ves. ad lib.

S. Baring-Gould, 1834–1924.

ONWARD, Christian soldiers!
　　Marching as to war,
With the cross of Jesus
　　Going on before.
Christ the royal Master
　　Leads against the foe;
Forward into battle,
　　See, his banners go:

Onward, Christian soldiers,
*　　Marching as to war,*
With the cross of Jesus
*　　Going on before.*

2 Like a mighty army
　　Moves the Church of God;
Brothers, we are treading
　　Where the saints have trod;
We are not divided,
　　All one body we,
One in hope and doctrine,
　　One in charity:

3 Crowns and thrones may perish,
　　Kingdoms rise and wane,
But the Church of Jesus
　　Constant will remain;
Gates of hell can never
　　'Gainst that Church prevail;

We have Christ's own promise,
　　And that cannot fail:

4 Onward, then, ye people,
　　Join our happy throng,
Blend with ours your voices
　　In the triumph song;
Glory, laud, and honour
　　Unto Christ the King;
This through countless ages
　　Men and angels sing:

Onward, Christian soldiers,
*　　Marching as to war,*
With the cross of Jesus
*　　Going on before.*

129

IN DER WIEGEN. (76. 76. D.)

Moderately slow.   Melody from CORNER's *Geistliche Nachtigall*, 1649.

P. Dearmer.

REMEMBER all the people
    Who live in far-off lands
In strange and lovely cities,
    Or roam the desert sands,
Or farm the mountain pastures,
    Or till the endless plains
Where children wade through rice-fields
    And watch the camel-trains:

2 Some work in sultry forests
    Where apes swing to and fro,
Some fish in mighty rivers,
    Some hunt across the snow.
Remember all God's children,
    Who yet have never heard
The truth that comes from Jesus,
    The glory of his word.

3 God bless the men and women
    Who serve him oversea;
God raise up more to help them
    To set the nations free,
Till all the distant people
    In every foreign place
Shall understand his Kingdom
    And come into his grace.

(148)

130

MORNING LIGHT. (7 6. 7 6. D.)

Brightly.

G. J. WEBB, 1803–87.

G. *Duffield*,† 1818–88.

STAND up, stand up for Jesus,
Ye soldiers of the cross!
Lift high his royal banner;
It must not suffer loss.
From victory unto victory
His army he shall lead,
Till every foe is vanquished,
And Christ is Lord indeed.

2 Stand up, stand up for Jesus!
Stand in his strength alone;
The arm of flesh will fail you,
Ye dare not trust your own.
Put on the Gospel armour,
Each piece put on with prayer;
Where duty calls or danger,
Be never wanting there!

3 Stand up, stand up for Jesus!
The strife will not be long;
This day the noise of battle,
The next the victor's song.
To him that overcometh
A crown of life shall be;
He with the King of Glory
Shall reign eternally.

131

OLD 81ST (OLD 77TH).   (D.C.M.)
Slow and dignified.

Este's Psalter, 1592.
Original version appeared in *Day's Psalter*, 1562.

Bishop R. Heber, 1783–1826.

THE Son of God goes forth to war,
    A kingly crown to gain;
His blood-red banner streams afar!
    Who follows in his train?
Who best can drink his cup of woe,
    Triumphant over pain,
Who patient bears his cross below,
    He follows in his train.

2 The Martyr first, whose eagle eye
    Could pierce beyond the grave;
Who saw his Master in the sky,
    And called on him to save.
Like him, with pardon on his tongue
    In midst of mortal pain,
He prayed for them that did the wrong!
    Who follows in his train?

3 A glorious band, the chosen few
    On whom the Spirit came,
Twelve valiant Saints, their hope they knew,
    And mocked the cross and flame.
They met the tyrant's brandish'd steel,
    The lion's gory mane,
They bowed their necks the death to feel;
    Who follows in their train?

4 A noble army, men and boys,
    The matron and the maid,
Around the Saviour's throne rejoice
    In robes of light arrayed.
They climbed the steep ascent of heaven
    Through peril, toil, and pain;
O God, to us may grace be given
    To follow in their train.

132

STOWEY. (7 4. 7 4. Irreg.)

In moderate time.   Adapted from an English Traditional Melody.

Jan Struther.

WHEN a knight won his spurs, in the stories of old,
He was gentle and brave, he was gallant and bold;
With a shield on his arm and a lance in his hand
For God and for valour he rode through the land.

2 No charger have I, and no sword by my side,
Yet still to adventure and battle I ride,
Though back into storyland giants have fled,
And the knights are no more and the dragons are dead.

3 Let faith be my shield and let joy be my steed
'Gainst the dragons of anger, the ogres of greed;
And let me set free, with the sword of my youth,
From the castle of darkness the power of the truth.

133

WAINWRIGHT. (L.M.)

In moderate time. Later form of melody by RICHARD WAINWRIGHT, 1758–1825.

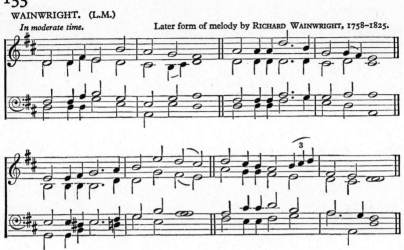

Rebecca J. Weston.

F ATHER, we thank thee for the night,
And for the pleasant morning light;
For rest and food and loving care,
And all that makes the day so fair.

2 Help us to do the things we should,
To be to others kind and good;
In all we do at work or play
To grow more loving every day.

134

BUNESSAN. (5 5. 5 4. D.)
In moderate time.

Old Gaelic Melody.

Thanks for a Day.   *Eleanor Farjeon.*

MORNING has broken
    Like the first morning,
Blackbird has spoken
    Like the first bird.
      Praise for the singing!
      Praise for the morning!
      Praise for them, springing
        Fresh from the Word!

2 Sweet the rain's new fall
    Sunlit from heaven,
Like the first dewfall
    On the first grass.
      Praise for the sweetness
      Of the wet garden,
      Sprung in completeness
        Where his feet pass.

3 Mine is the sunlight!
    Mine is the morning
Born of the one light
    Eden saw play!
      Praise with elation,
      Praise every morning,
      God's re-creation
        Of the new day!

135

HARDWICK.   (6 5. 6 5. D.   Irregular.)

In moderate time.

English Traditional Melody.

[*Copyright, 1925, by R. Vaughan Williams.*]

Thomas Carlyle, 1795–1881.

SO here hath been dawning
  Another blue day:
Think, wilt thou let it
  Slip useless away?

2 Out of eternity
  This new day is born;
Into eternity,
  At night, will return.

3 Behold it aforetime
  No eye ever did:
So soon it forever
  From all eyes is hid.

4 Here hath been dawning
  Another blue day:
Think, wilt thou let it
  Slip useless away?

136

MELCOMBE. (L.M.)
Moderately slow.

S. WEBBE (the elder), 1740–1816.

Descant (Melody in the Tenor).

MARTIN SHAW.

J. *Keble*, 1792–1866.

NEW every morning is the love
  Our wakening and uprising prove;
Through sleep and darkness safely brought,
Restored to life, and power, and thought.

(Descant) 2 New mercies, each returning day,
  Hover around us while we pray;
  New perils past, new sins forgiven,
  New thoughts of God, new hopes of heaven.

  3 If on our daily course our mind
  Be set to hallow all we find,
  New treasures still, of countless price,
  God will provide for sacrifice.

(*Descant*) 4 The trivial round, the common task,
  Would furnish all we ought to ask,—
  Room to deny ourselves, a road
  To bring us daily nearer God.

5 Only, O Lord, in thy dear love
  Fit us for perfect rest above;
  And help us this and every day
  To live more nearly as we pray.

137

GARDEN. (10. 10.)
In moderate time. Adapted from an English Traditional Melody.

[*Copyright, 1929, by Oxford University Press.*]

Based on Robert Herrick, 1591–1674.

WHEN virgin morn doth call thee to arise,
  Come thus in sober joy to sacrifice:

2 First wash thy heart in innocence, then bring
  Pure hands, pure habits; make pure everything.

3 Next humbly kneel before God's throne, and thence
  Give up thy soul in clouds of frankincense.

4 Censers of gold, thus filled with odours sweet,
  Shall make thy actions with their ends to meet.

138

TALLIS' CANON. (L.M.)

Slow and dignified.

T. TALLIS, *c.* 1510–85.

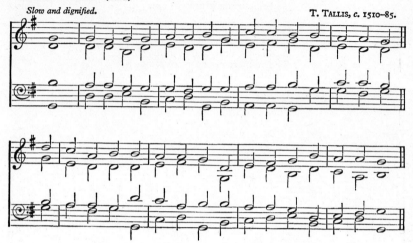

Bishop T. Ken, 1637–1711.

Glory to thee, my God, this night
For all the blessings of the light;
Keep me, O keep me, King of Kings,
Beneath thy own almighty wings.

(Descant) 2 Forgive me, Lord, for thy dear Son,
The ill that I this day have done,
That with the world, myself, and thee,
I, ere I sleep, at peace may be.

3 Teach me to live, that I may dread
The grave as little as my bed;
Teach me to die, that so I may
Rise glorious at the aweful day.

(Descant) 4 O may my soul on thee repose,
And with sweet sleep mine eyelids close,
Sleep that may me more vigorous make
To serve my God when I awake.

5 Praise God, from whom all blessings flow;
Praise him, all creatures here below;
Praise him above, ye heavenly host;
Praise Father, Son, and Holy Ghost.

A-men.

(158)

138 (cont.) ALTERNATIVE VERSION (for verses 2 and 4).

MELODY.

Fa-burden from *Ravenscroft's Psalter*, 1621.

DESCANT.

139

AR HYD Y NOS. (8 4. 8 4. 8 8. 8 4.)

In moderate time.

Welsh Traditional Melody.

1. *Bishop Heber* (1827).
2. *Archbishop Whately‡* (1855).

GOD, that madest earth and heaven,
    Darkness and light;
Who the day for toil hast given,
    For rest the night;
May thine angel-guards defend us,
Slumber sweet thy mercy send us,
Holy dreams and hopes attend us,
    This livelong night.

2 Guard us waking, guard us sleeping;
    And, when we die,
May we in thy mighty keeping
    All peaceful lie:
So when death to life shall wake us,
Thou may'st like the angels make us,
And to reign in glory take us
    With thee on high.

140

EUDOXIA. (6 5. 6 5.)

Moderately slow.

S. BARING-GOULD, 1834–1924;

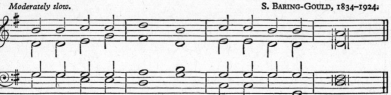

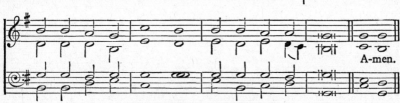

A-men.

[*By permission of A. W. Ridley & Co.*]

S. *Baring-Gould*, 1834–1924.

NOW the day is over,
 Night is drawing nigh,
Shadows of the evening
 Steal across the sky.

2 Now the darkness gathers,
 Stars begin to peep,
Birds and beasts and flowers
 Soon will be asleep.

3 Jesus, give the weary
 Calm and sweet repose;
With thy tenderest blessing
 May our eyelids close.

4 Grant to little children
 Visions bright of thee;
Guard the sailors tossing
 On the deep blue sea.

5 Comfort every sufferer
 Watching late in pain;
Those who plan some evil
 From their sin restrain.

*6 Through the long night watches
 May thine angels spread
Their white wings above me,
 Watching round my bed.

*7 When the morning wakens,
 Then may I arise
Pure, and fresh, and sinless
 In thy holy eyes.

8 Glory to the Father,
 Glory to the Son,
And to thee, blest Spirit,
 Whilst all ages run.

(161)

M

141

ARNSTADT (SEELENBRÄUTIGAM). (5 5. 8 8. 5 5.)

Slow.

A. DRESE, 1620–1701.

W. Romanis, 1824–99.

ROUND me falls the night;
Saviour, be my light:
Through the hours in darkness shrouded
Let me see thy face unclouded;
Let thy glory shine
In this heart of mine.

2 Earthly work is done,
Earthly sounds are none;
Rest in sleep and silence seeking,
Let me hear thee softly speaking;
In my spirit's ear
Whisper, 'I am near.'

3 Blessèd, heavenly Light,
Shining through earth's night;
Voice, that oft of love hast told me;
Arms, so strong to clasp and hold me;
Thou thy watch wilt keep,
Saviour, o'er my sleep.

142

BIRLING. (L.M.)

Not too slow.

Arranged by GEOFFREY SHAW,
from an early 19th cent. MS.

J. Keble, 1792–1866.

SUN of my soul, thou Saviour dear,
It is not night if thou be near:
O may no earth-born cloud arise
To hide thee from thy servant's eyes.

2 When the soft dews of kindly sleep
My wearied eyelids gently steep,
Be my last thought, how sweet to rest
For ever on my Saviour's breast.

3 Abide with me from morn till eve,
For without thee I cannot live;
Abide with me when night is nigh,
For without thee I dare not die.

4 If some poor wandering child of thine
Have spurned to-day the voice divine,
Now, Lord, the gracious work begin;
Let him no more lie down in sin.

5 Watch by the sick; enrich the poor
With blessings from thy boundless store;
Be every mourner's sleep to-night
Like infant's slumbers, pure and light.

6 Come near and bless us when we wake,
Ere through the world our way we take;
Till in the ocean of thy love
We lose ourselves in heaven above.

143

INNSBRUCK. (7 7 6. 7 7 8.) Traditional German Melody, possibly by H. ISAAK (c. 1490).
Slow and solemn. Adapted and harmonized by J. S. BACH.

Y. H., *based on* Nun ruhen alle Wälder. P. Gerhardt, 1607–76.

THE duteous day now closeth,
  Each flower and tree reposeth,
    Shade creeps o'er wild and wood:
Let us, as night is falling,
On God our maker calling,
    Give thanks to him, the giver good.

2 Now all the heavenly splendour
  Breaks forth in starlight tender
    From myriad worlds unknown;
And man, the marvel seeing,
Forgets his selfish being,
    For joy of beauty not his own.

3 His care he drowneth yonder,
  Lost in the abyss of wonder;
    To heaven his soul doth steal:
This life he disesteemeth,
The day it is that dreameth,
    That doth from truth his vision seal.

4. Awhile his mortal blindness
  May miss God's loving-kindness,
    And grope in faithless strife:
But when life's day is over
Shall death's fair night discover
    The fields of everlasting life.

144

BUTLER. (C.M.)

Not too fast.

English Traditional Melody.

M. M. Penstone,† 1859–1910.

WHEN lamps are lighted in the town,
　　The boats sail out to sea;
The fishers watch when night comes down,
　　They work for you and me.

2 When little children go to rest,
　　Before they sleep, they pray
That God will bless the fishermen
　　And bring them back at day.

3 The boats come in at early dawn,
　　When children wake in bed;
Upon the beach the boats are drawn,
　　And all the nets are spread.

4 God hath watched o'er the fishermen
　　Far on the deep dark sea,
And brought them safely home again,
　　Where they are glad to be.

145 LOUGHBOROUGH. (7 6. 7 6. D.)

In moderate time.

G. W. BRIGGS.

[*Copyright, 1925, by Oxford University Press.*]

G. W. Briggs.

OUR Father, by whose servants
　Our house was built of old,
Whose hand hath crowned her children
　With blessings manifold,
For thine unfailing mercies
　Far-strewn along our way,
With all who passed before us,
　We praise thy name to-day.

2 The changeful years unresting
　Their silent course have sped,
New comrades ever bringing
　In comrades' steps to tread;
And some are long forgotten,
　Long spent their hopes and fears:
Safe rest they in thy keeping,
　Who changest not with years.

(166)

3 They reap not where they laboured,
　　We reap what they have sown;
　Our harvest may be garnered
　　By ages yet unknown.
　The days of old have dowered us
　　With gifts beyond all praise:
　Our Father, make us faithful
　　To serve the coming days.

4 Before us and beside us,
　　Still holden in thine hand,
　A cloud unseen of witness,
　　Our elder comrades stand:
　One family unbroken,
　　We join, with one acclaim,
　One heart, one voice uplifting,
　　To glorify thy name.

Descant to verse 2 or 3 (or verses 2 and 3). Accompaniment as before. 　　MARTIN SHAW.

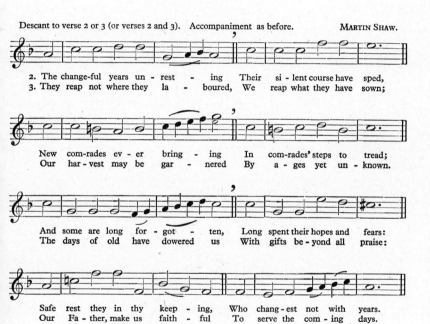

2. The change-ful years un - rest - ing　Their　si - lent course have sped,
3. They reap not where they　la - boured, We　reap what they have sown;

New com-rades ev - er　bring - ing　In com-rades' steps to tread;
Our har - vest may be gar - nered By a - ges yet un - known.

And some are long for - got - ten, Long spent their hopes and fears:
The days of old have dowered us　With gifts be - yond all praise:

Safe rest they in thy keep - ing, Who chang-est not with years.
Our Fa - ther, make us faith - ful To serve the com - ing days.

Loughborough School Hymn (adapted, by permission).

(NOTE.—*Schools with a known founder may prefer, in verse 1, the original version—'servant'; and ancient
foundations may prefer the original of verse 2.*

Four hundred years enduring,
　From age to following age,
A hundred generations
　Have built our heritage:
Their name is long forgotten,
　Long spent their hopes and fears:
Safe rest they in thy keeping,
　Who changest not with years.)

(Continued overleaf)

145 (*cont.*)

(Or verse 3 may be sung in three parts unaccompanied, or with the accompaniment below.)

1ST TREBLE.   MARTIN SHAW.

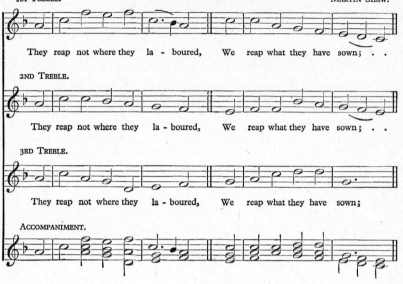

They reap not where they la - boured, We reap what they have sown; . .

2ND TREBLE.

They reap not where they la - boured, We reap what they have sown; . .

3RD TREBLE.

They reap not where they la - boured, We reap what they have sown;

ACCOMPANIMENT.

1ST TREBLE.

Our har - vest may be gar - nered By ag - es yet un - known.

2ND TREBLE.

Our har - vest may be gar - nered By ag - es yet un - known.

3RD TREBLE.

Our har - vest may be gar - nered By ag - es yet un - known.

ACCOMPANIMENT.

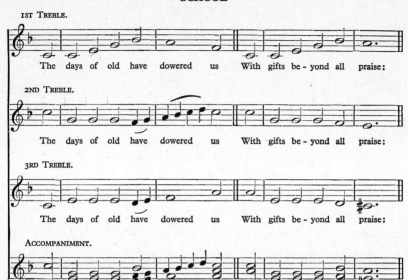

1ST TREBLE.

The days of old have dowered us With gifts be-yond all praise:

2ND TREBLE.

The days of old have dowered us With gifts be-yond all praise:

3RD TREBLE.

The days of old have dowered us With gifts be-yond all praise:

ACCOMPANIMENT.

1ST TREBLE.

Our Fa-ther, make us faith-ful To serve the com-ing days.

2ND TREBLE.

Our Fa-ther, make us faith-ful To serve the com-ing days.

3RD TREBLE.

Our Fa-ther, make us faith-ful To serve the com-ing days.

ACCOMPANIMENT.

Where this three-part setting is attempted, it may be found convenient to separate the voices, from the beginning, into three sections. All voices will join in verse 1; sections 1 and 2 in verse 2; sections 1, 2, 3 in verse 3; and again all voices in unison for verse 4.

It will be observed that each part in turn picks up the melody of the original tune.

146

DISMISSAL. (8 7. 8 7. 8 7.)

In moderate time.

W. L. VINER, 1790–1867.

H. J. Buckoll, 1803–71.

Assembly.

LORD, behold us with thy blessing,
   Once again assembled here;
Onward be our footsteps pressing,
   In thy love and faith and fear:
      Still protect us
   By thy presence ever near.

2 For thy mercy we adore thee,
   For this rest upon our way;
Lord, again we bow before thee,
   Speed our labours day by day:
      Mind and spirit
   With thy choicest gifts array.

Dismissal.

1 Lord, dismiss us with thy blessing;
   Thanks for mercies past receive;
Pardon all, their faults confessing;
   Time that 's lost may all retrieve:
      May thy children
   Ne'er again thy Spirit grieve.

2 Let thy Father-hand be shielding
   All who here shall meet no more;
May their seed-time past be yielding
   Year by year a richer store:
      Those returning
   Make more faithful than before.

147

RANDOLPH. (9 8. 8 9.)

In moderate time. Unison. *Harmony.* R. Vaughan Williams.

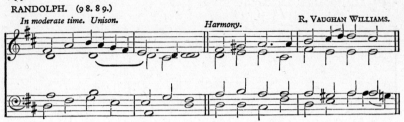

Unison.

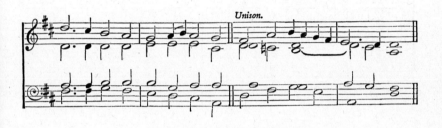

J. E. Rankin, 1828–1904.

GOD be with you till we meet again;
By his counsels guide, uphold you,
With his sheep securely fold you:
God be with you till we meet again.

2 God be with you till we meet again;
'Neath his wings protecting hide you,
Daily manna still provide you:
God be with you till we meet again.

3 God be with you till we meet again;
When life's perils thick confound you,
Put his arm unfailing round you:
God be with you till we meet again.

4 God be with you till we meet again;
Keep love's banner floating o'er you,
Smite death's threatening wave before you:
God be with you till we meet again.

148 LLANGOLLEN (LLEDROD). (L.M.)

With vigour.

Welsh Hymn Melody.

Rudyard Kipling.

Land of our birth, we pledge to thee
Our love and toil in the years to be;
When we are grown and take our place,
As men and women with our race.

FATHER in Heaven who lovest all,
O help thy children when they call,
That they may build from age to age
An undefilèd heritage.

2 Teach us to bear the yoke in youth,
With steadfastness and careful truth;
That, in our time thy grace may give
The truth whereby the nations live.

3 Teach us to rule ourselves alway,
Controlled and cleanly night and day;
That we may bring, if need arise,
No maimed or worthless sacrifice.

4 Teach us to look in all our ends
On thee for judge, and not our friends;
That we, with thee, may walk uncowed
By fear or favour of the crowd.

5 Teach us the strength that cannot seek,
By deed or thought, to hurt the weak;
That, under thee, we may possess
Man's strength to comfort man's distress.

6 Teach us delight in simple things,
And mirth that has no bitter springs;
Forgiveness free of evil done,
And love to all men 'neath the sun.

Land of our birth, our faith, our pride,
For whose dear sake our fathers died;
O Motherland, we pledge to thee,
Head, heart, and hand through the years to be!

149

NATIONAL ANTHEM. (6 6 4. 6 6 6 4.)

Moderately slow.   Source unknown.

National Anthem.

GOD save our gracious King,
 Long live our noble King,
  God save the King!
Send him victorious,
Happy and glorious,
Long to reign over us;
  God save the King!

The Motherland.

2 One realm of races four,
  Blest ever more and more,
    God save our land!

Home of the brave and free,
Set in the silver sea,
True nurse of chivalry,
  God save our land!

The Empire.

3 Of many a race and birth,
  One Empire, wide as earth,
    As ocean wide,
  Brothers in war and peace,
  Brothers, that war may cease;
  God, who hath given increase,
    Still guard and guide.

(On general occasions the following version of v. 3 may be preferred.)

Of many a race and birth
From utmost ends of earth,
  God save us all!
Bid strife and hatred cease,
Bid hope and joy increase,
Spread universal peace,
  God save us all!

*(For Empire Day and similar occasions see also 109, 148; and for Armistice Day also
86, 87, 90, 123–132.)*

GRACE BEFORE MEALS

I

PACHELBEL (WAS GOTT THUT.) (88. 8 8 8.)

Rather slow.

G. W. Briggs.

? J. PACHELBEL, 1653–1706.

1. Our Fa - ther, for our dai - ly bread Ac - cept our praise and hear our prayer. By thee all liv - ing souls are fed: Thy boun - ty and thy lov - ing care With all thy chil - dren let us share.

2

To be sung to BATTISHILL, 71.

E. Rutter Leatham.

THANK you for the world so sweet;
Thank you for the food we eat;
Thank you for the birds that sing:
Thank you, God, for everything!

(174)

AMEN

(Most of the following, being in the same key, may be combined in one service.)

(The second treble may be sung alone; or parts two and three together; or all three parts.)

CAROLS

Christmas and after

I

PUER NATUS

In moderate time.

Melody from L. Lossius's
Psalmodia, 1553.

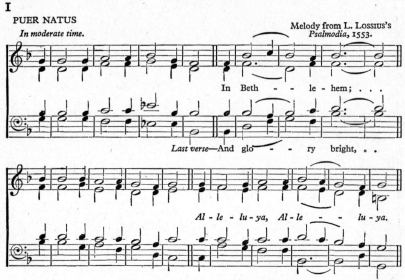

In Beth - - le - hem; . . .

Last verse—And glo - - ry bright, . .

Al - le - lu - ya, Al - le - - lu - ya.

German, 16th century. Tr. N. S. T.

A BOY was born in Bethlehem;
   Rejoice for that, Jerusalem!
    Alleluya.

2 For low he lay within a stall,
   Who rules for ever over all:

3 He let himself a servant be,
   That all mankind he might set free:

4 Then praise the Word of God who
      came,
   To dwell within a human frame:

5 And praised be God in threefold might,
    And glory bright,
   Eternal, good, and infinite!

2

IRIS. (8 7. 8 7. and refrain.)

In moderate time.

French Carol Melody.

J. *Montgomery*, 1771–1854.

ANGELS, from the realms of glory,
  Wing your flight o'er all the earth;
Ye who sang creation's story
  Now proclaim Messiah's birth:

  Come and worship
    Christ, the new-born King.
  Come and worship,
    Worship Christ, the new-born King.

2 Shepherds in the fields abiding,
    Watching o'er your flocks by night,
  God with man is now residing;
    Yonder shines the infant Light:

3 Sages, leave your contemplations;
    Brighter visions beam afar;
  Seek the great Desire of Nations;
    Ye have seen his natal star:

*4 Saints before the altar bending,
    Watching long in hope and fear,
  Suddenly the Lord, descending,
    In his temple shall appear:

5 Though an infant now we view him,
    He shall fill his Father's throne,
  Gather all the nations to him;
    Every knee shall then bow down:

  Come and worship
    Christ, the new-born King.
  Come and worship,
    Worship Christ, the new-born King.

N

3

THE BIRDS. (102. 102. 8 8 6.)

Rather quick.

Czech Traditional Carol.

[*Copyright, 1928, by Martin Shaw.*]
(*This may be sung without chorus and solo.*)

The Birds Carol.

O. B. C. from the Czech.

FROM out of a wood did a cuckoo fly,
Cuckoo,
He came to a manger with joyful cry,
Cuckoo;
He hopped, he curtsied, round he flew,
And loud his jubilation grew,
Cuckoo, cuckoo, cuckoo.

2 A pigeon flew over to Galilee,
Vrercroo,
He strutted, and cooed, and was full of glee,
Vrercroo,
And showed with jewelled wings unfurled,
His joy that Christ was in the world,
Vrercroo, vrercroo, vrercroo.

3. A dove settled down upon Nazareth,
       Tsucroo,
And tenderly chanted with all his breath,
      Tsucroo:
'O you,' he cooed, 'so good and true,
My beauty do I give to you—
    Tsucroo, tsucroo, tsucroo.'

4

NORTHUMBRIA. (8 7. 8 7.)

Moderately slow.

Verse 1.   English Traditional Melody.

Verses 2 and 4.   *1st time.*   *2nd time.*

Verse 3 may be sung in two parts: the piano or organ playing the accompaniment. The original melody is now written in the tenor.

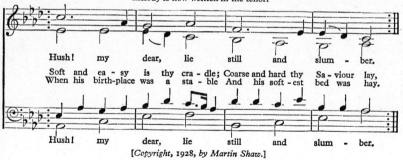

Hush! my   dear, lie still and slum - ber.

Soft and ea - sy is thy cra - dle; Coarse and hard thy Sa - viour lay,
When his birth-place was a sta - ble And his soft - est bed was hay.

Hush! my   dear, lie still and slum - ber.

[*Copyright, 1928, by Martin Shaw.*]

(*Or verses 2 and 4 may be sung in this way.*)

Cradle Song.   *Isaac Watts,* 1674–1748.

HUSH! my dear, lie still and slumber;
  Holy angels guard thy bed!
Heavenly blessings without number
  Gently falling on thy head.

2 How much better thou'rt attended
  Than the Son of God could be
When from heaven he descended,
  And became a child like thee.

3 Soft and easy is thy cradle;
  Coarse and hard thy Saviour lay,
When his birthplace was a stable
  And his softest bed was hay.

4. May'st thou live to know and fear him,
  Trust and love him all thy days:
Then go dwell for ever near him,
  See his face and sing his praise.

5

GOD REST YOU MERRY.

In moderate time.

English Traditional Carol Tune.

And it's ti - dings of com - fort and joy, com-fort and joy: And it's ti - dings of com — fort and joy. joy.

Last verse.

CAROLS

GOD rest you merry, gentlemen,
  Let nothing you dismay,
Remember Christ our Saviour
  Was born on Christmas Day,
To save poor souls from Satan's power
  Which had long time gone astray,
And it's tidings of comfort and joy.

2 From God that is our Father,
    The blessèd angels came,
  Unto some certain shepherds,
    With tidings of the same;
  That there was born in Bethlehem,
    The Son of God by name.
  And it's tidings of comfort and joy.

3 Go, fear not, said God's angels,
    Let nothing you affright,
  For there is born in Bethlehem,
    Of a pure Virgin bright,
  One able to advance you,
    And throw down Satan quite.
  And it's tidings of comfort and joy.

4 The shepherds at those tidings
    Rejoicèd much in mind,
  And left their flocks a feeding
    In tempest storms of wind,
  And straight they came to Bethlehem,
    The Son of God to find.
  And it's tidings of comfort and joy.

5 Now when they came to Bethlehem,
    Where our sweet Saviour lay,
  They found him in a manger,
    Where oxen feed on hay,
  The blessèd Virgin kneeling down,
    Unto the Lord did pray.
  And it's tidings of comfort and joy.

6 With sudden joy and gladness,
    The shepherds were beguiled,
  To see the Babe of Israel
    Before his mother mild,
  On them with joy and cheerfulness
    Rejoice each mother's child.
  And it's tidings of comfort and joy.

          (*Before Christmas only.*)
7 Now to the Lord sing praises,
    All you within this place,
  Like we true loving brethren,
    Each other to embrace,
  For the merry time of Christmas,
    Is drawing on apace.
  And it's tidings of comfort and joy.

('*God rest you merry*' means '*God keep you merry*'.)

6

A GALLERY CAROL.
Moderately fast.

*Words and music from an old
Dorset Church-gallery book.*

Church-gallery Book.

REJOICE and be merry in songs and in mirth!
O praise our Redeemer, all mortals on earth!
For this is the birthday of Jesus our King,
Who brought us salvation—his praises we'll sing!

2 A heavenly vision appeared in the sky;
Vast numbers of angels the Shepherds did spy,
Proclaiming the birthday of Jesus our King,
Who brought us salvation—his praises we'll sing!

3 Likewise a bright star in the sky did appear,
Which led the Wise Men from the east to draw near;
They found the Messiah, sweet Jesus our King,
Who brought us salvation—his praises we'll sing!

4 And when they were come, they their treasures unfold,
And unto him offered myrrh, incense, and gold.
So blessèd for ever be Jesus our King,
Who brought us salvation—his praises we'll sing!

7

EIA, EIA (ZU BETHLEHEM GEBOREN).
(7 6. 7 6. 4 6.)

Moderately slow.

Melody from NORDSTERN'S *Führer zur Seligkeit,* 1671.

Eia.   *Cölner Psalter,* 1638.   *Pr. O. B. C.*

TO us in Bethlehem city
　Was born a little son;
In him all gentle graces
　Were gathered into one,
　　Eia, Eia,
　Were gathered into one.

2 And all our love and fortune
　Lie in his mighty hands;
Our sorrows, joys, and failures,
　He sees and understands,
　　Eia, Eia,
　He sees and understands.

3 O Shepherd ever near us,
　We'll go where thou dost lead;
No matter where the pasture,
　With thee at hand to feed,
　　Eia, Eia,
　With thee at hand to feed.

4 No grief shall part us from thee,
　However sharp the edge:
We'll serve, and do thy bidding—
　O take our hearts in pledge!
　　Eia, Eia,
　Take thou our hearts in pledge!

(Eia *is a Latin exclamation of joy, and is pronounced* '*ïyah*'.)

8

THREE KINGS

In moderate time.

J. H. Hopkins, 1820–91.
J. H. Hopkins, Jun. (arr. M. S.).

1. THE THREE KINGS. 5. ALL VOICES, *Unison, as in Melody Edition.*

1 We three kings of O - ri - ent are; Bear - ing gifts we tra - verse a - far
5. Glo - rious now, be - hold him a - rise, King, and God, and sac - ri - fice!

These two verses (either or both) may be sung in three parts, the 1st treble as above.

2ND TREBLE.

1 We three kings of O - ri - ent are; Bear - ing gifts we tra - verse a - far
5. Glo - rious now, be - hold him a - rise, King, and God, and sac - ri - fice!

3RD TREBLE.

Field and foun - tain, moor and moun - tain, Fol - low - ing yon - der star:
Heaven sings al - le - lu - ya, Al - le - lu - ya the earth re - plies:

Field and foun - tain, moor and moun - tain, Fol - low - ing yon - der star:
Heaven sings al - le - lu - ya, Al - le - lu - ya the earth re - plies:

REFRAIN (after each verse).

O star of won-der, star of night, Star with roy-al beau-ty bright,

West-ward lead-ing, still pro-ceed-ing, Guide us to thy per-fect light.

INTERLUDE.

(Fl. or Ob.)

(Clar.)

vv. 2, 3, 4. Accompaniment as before.

MELCHIOR.
2 Born a king on Beth-le-hem plain, Gold I

GASPAR.
3 Frank-in-cense to of-fer have I; In-cense

BALTHAZAR.
4 Myrrh is mine; its bit-ter per-fume Breathes a

bring, to crown him a-gain— King for ev-er,
owns a De-i-ty nigh: Prayer and prais-ing,
life of gath-er-ing gloom; Sorrow-ing, sigh-ing,

ceas-ing nev-er, Ov-er us all to reign:
all men rais-ing, Wor-ship him, God most high:
bleed-ing, dy-ing, Sealed in the stone-cold tomb:

For verse 5 go back to the beginning.

9

SANS DAY.
In moderate time.

English Traditional Carol Melody.

Cornish.

Now the holly bears a berry as white as the milk,
And Mary bore Jesus, who was wrapped up in silk:

And Mary bore Jesus Christ our Saviour for to be,
And the first tree in the greenwood, it was the holly, holly, holly!
And the first tree in the greenwood, it was the holly.

2 Now the holly bears a berry as green as the grass,
And Mary bore Jesus, who died on the cross:

3 Now the holly bears a berry as black as the coal,
And Mary bore Jesus, who died for us all:

4 Now the holly bears a berry, as blood is it red,
Then trust we our Saviour, who rose from the dead:

The Sans Day or St. Day Carol has been so named because the melody and the first three verses were
taken down at St. Day in the parish of Gwennap, Cornwall. St. Day or St. They was a Breton saint
whose cult was widely spread in Armorican Cornwall. We owe the carol to the kindness of the Rev.
G. H. Doble, to whom Mr. W. D. Watson sang it after hearing an old man, Mr. Thomas Beard, sing it
at St. Day. A version in Cornish was subsequently published ('Ma gron war'n gelinen') with a fourth
stanza, here translated and added to Mr. Beard's English version.

10

VICTOR KING (CHRISTUS IST ERSTANDEN). (7 8. 8 8. 8 8.)

Rather quick.

German Carol. Melody from the Trier *Gesangbuch*, 1871.

Jan Struther.

ROUND the earth a message runs:
Awake, awake, you drowsy ones!
Now leaps the sap in every stem
To chant the winter's requiem.
No more of sloth and dullness sing:
Sing love, sing joy, for Christ is King!

2 Round the earth a message runs:
Arise, arise, you doleful ones!
Cast off your chains, you captives all
Who long have lain in sorrow's thrall.
No more of grief and anguish sing:
Sing love, sing joy, for Christ is King!

3 Round the earth a message runs:
For shame, for shame, you brawling ones!
You shall more true adventure find
In friendliness of heart and mind.
No more of hate and envy sing:
Sing love, sing joy, for Christ is King!

4 Round the earth a message runs:
Rejoice, rejoice, you happy ones!
Now fall the gods of wrath and pain,
Now comes your Prince of Joy to reign;
To him your brave allegiance sing:
Sing love, sing joy, for Christ is King!

(See also Hymns 95, 96.)

INDEX OF FIRST LINES

MUSICAL SETTINGS

TO

PRAYERS AND THANKSGIVINGS

AND

CHANTS

*For convenience of use with 'Prayers and Hymns for
Junior Schools', these musical settings are arranged under
the days of the week, as in that book. For other use there
is an Index in alphabetical order, see p. 223.
For Index of Chants, see p. 224.*

GOD BE IN MY HEAD

DAVID. (Irregular.)

Rather slow.

G. W. BRIGGS.

1. God be in my head, And in my un - der - stand - ing;

2. God be in mine eyes, And in my look - ing; 3. God be in my

mouth, And in my speak - ing; 4. God be in my heart, And in my

Rather more slowly and quietly. rall. . . . .

think - ing; 5. God be at mine end, And at my de - part - ing.

[Copyright, 1929, by Oxford University Press.]

Sarum Primer, 1558.

IN GOD, WHO MADE US

Melody by G. W. Briggs.
Descant by Gordon Slater.

Optional Descant.

In God, who made us, God who keeps us,

Melody.

In God, who made us, God who keeps us,

Optional Descant.

Whose love will nev - er fail ... us,

Melody.

Whose love will nev - er fail ... us,

All voices in unison.

In him will we trust for ev - - er.

The above is complete in itself: but the following Amen may be added, or sung separately:

Optional Descant.

Gordon Slater.

A - - - - - - - men.

Melody.

A - - - - - - - men.

(The melody may be sung in unison throughout.)

(193)

O

NOW ARE WE THE SONS OF GOD

Allegro moderato. ♩=about 66.   MARTIN SHAW.

Now are we the sons of God, now are we the sons of God, and it

Now are we the sons of God, now are we the sons of

doth not yet ap - pear what we shall be: But we

God, and it doth not yet ap - pear what we shall be:

1ST TREBLE.

know   that we shall be like him,   that we shall be like

2ND TREBLE.

For we know   that we shall be like him,   that

PIANO OR ORGAN.

1ST TREBLE.

f   *poco rit.*

him: for we shall see   him   as   he   is.

2ND TREBLE.

f   *poco rit.*

we shall be like   him: for we shall see him   as   he   is.

PIANO OR ORGAN.

poco rit.

f

It should be explained to the children that the above is a canon at the unison.

ALMIGHTY GOD, WHOSE SERVICE IS PERFECT FREEDOM

In moderate time.   Unison.   R. Vaughan Williams.

Al - migh - ty   God,   whose   ser - vice   is   per - fect

free - dom: grant us   so . . . .   to   fol - low the ex-

- am - ple of thy Son Je - sus Christ,   that we may find our

joy   in   ser - vice, all the days of   our   life.   A - - - men.

GOD BE MERCIFUL UNTO US AND BLESS US

GORDON SLATER.

(The Melody only may be sung.)

O GOD, GRANT ME THIS DAY

R. VAUGHAN WILLIAMS.

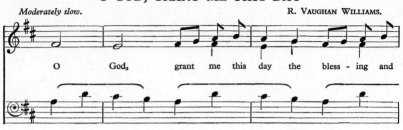

O God, grant me this day the bless - ing and

help of thy Ho - ly Spi - rit: .... through Je - sus

Christ our Lord. A - - - - - - men.

Ped.

SURSUM CORDA

(The teacher's part may, if the teacher prefers, be sung on one note only, or said.)

To be sung lightly and in the rhythm of speech.

G. W. BRIGGS and GORDON SLATER.

Lift up your hearts:

We lift them up un - to the Lord.

Let us give thanks un - to our Lord God:

It is meet and right so to do.

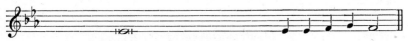

It is very meet, right, and our bounden duty, that we
should at all times, and in all places, give thanks unto
thee O Lord, Holy Father, Almighty, ...

Ev - er - last - ing God.

(199)

(This may be sung by a semi-choir.)

There-fore with An-gels and Arch-an-gels, and with all the com-pan - y of heaven,

we laud and mag - ni - fy thy glo - rious Name;

ev - er - more praising thee, and say - ing,

(A slight pause : then all voices.)

SANCTUS

G. W. BRIGGS and GORDON SLATER.

THANKSGIVINGS

G. W. BRIGGS and GORDON SLATER.

For the Church on earth and the Church in heaven: We praise thee, O God.

For the multitude which no man can number, of all nations and tongues, standing before the throne: We praise thee, O God.

For prophets and leaders and heroes of olden days: We praise thee, O God.

For all who are seeking, in this our day, to do thy will: We praise thee, O God.

For our fellowship with one another: for our opportunities of brave adventure in the name of Christ: We thank thee, O God.

ETERNAL FATHER, WHO HAST CALLED US

In free rhythm.   R. Vaughan Williams.

PRAISE THE LORD, O MY SOUL

With spirit = ♩about 144.

MARTIN SHAW.

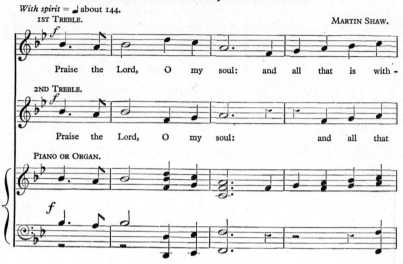

Praise the Lord, O my soul: and all that is with-

Praise the Lord, O my soul: and all that

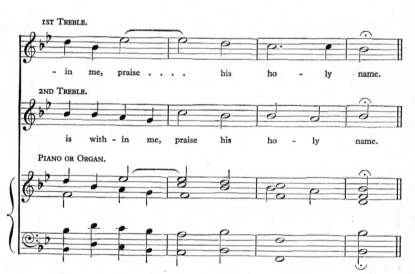

- in me, praise . . . . his ho - ly name.

is with - in me, praise his ho - ly name.

(The second treble part may be omitted, and the first treble sung by all voices.)

(The following Amen may be added.)

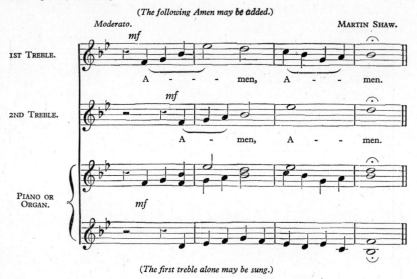

(The first treble alone may be sung.)

Friday I

DEAR FATHER, KEEP ME THROUGH THIS DAY

STRASSBURG. (C.M.)

Not too slow. Unison.   Melody from the *Strassburger Kirchengesang-Buch*, 1616.

Morning.   G. W. B.

DEAR Father, keep me through this day
    Obedient, kind and true:
That, always loving thee, I may
    Seek all thy will to do.

THE EARTH SHALL BE FULL OF THE KNOWLEDGE

(The first treble only may be sung.)

GLORIA IN EXCELSIS

GORDON SLATER.

Con moto.

1ST TREBLE.

Glo - ry be to God on high:

2ND TREBLE.

Glo - ry be to God on high:

Con moto.

PIANO OR ORGAN.

1ST TREBLE.

And in earth . . peace, . . good will towards men.

2ND TREBLE.

And in earth . . peace, good will towards men.

PIANO OR ORGAN.

(The first treble alone may be sung.)

HOLY FATHER, CHEER OUR WAY

TON-MÂN. (7 7 7. 5.)

In moderate time.

DAVID EVANS (adapted by permission).

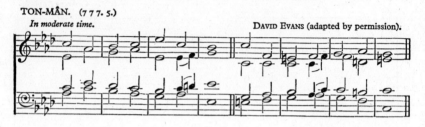

R. H. Robinson, 1842–92.

HOLY Father, cheer our way
With thy love's perpetual ray;
Grant us every closing day
Light at evening time.

Evening (suitable also for Morning)
I BIND UNTO MYSELF TO-DAY

ST. PATRICK.   (D.L.M.)
Slow and dignified.   From an Ancient Irish Hymn Melody.

St. Patrick's Breastplate.   St. Patrick, c. 372–466.   Tr. Mrs. C. F. Alexander.

O GOD, USE THE LOVE THAT IS IN ME

Andante con moto. ♩=54.

MARTIN SHAW.

O God, use the love that is in me, that is from

thee, for thee; O God, use the love that is in me, the love that is in

me, that is from thee, for thee . . . .

DAY BY DAY

STONETHWAITE. (3 8. 6 5. 6 3.)

Rather slow.

ARTHUR SOMERVELL.

St. Richard of Chichester, c. 1197–1253.

DAY by day,
  Dear Lord, of thee three things I pray:
    To see thee more clearly,
    Love thee more dearly,
    Follow thee more nearly,
      Day by day.

ENRICH, LORD, HEART, MOUTH, HANDS IN ME

WULFRUN. (8 8 8.)

In moderate time.

G. W. BRIGGS.

Descant by MARTIN SHAW.

(continued)

That I may run, rise, rest with thee.

I may run, rise, rest with thee.

George Herbert.†

DEAR GOD, BE GOOD TO ME

(A prayer of the Breton Fishermen.)

Moderately slow.

G. W. BRIGGS.

mp Dear God, be good to me. The sea is so

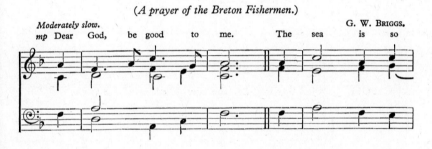

wide, and my boat is so small.

Accompaniment by J. H. Arnold.

Lift up your hearts:

We lift them up un-to the Lord.

Let us give thanks un-to our Lord God.

It is meet and right so to do.

It is very meet, right, and our bounden duty, that we should at all times, and in

all pla-ces, give thanks un-to thee, O Lord, Ho-ly

Fa - ther, Al - might - y, Ev - er - last - ing God.

There - fore with angels and archangels, and with all the company

of heaven, we laud and magnify thy glo - ri - ous Name;

ev - er - more prais - ing thee, and say - ing,

Ho - ly, . . ho - ly, . . ho - ly, . . Lord God of hosts, hea - ven and earth are

full of thy glo - ry. Glo-ry be to thee, O Lord most high. A - men.

NOW UNTO THE KING ETERNAL

G. W. BRIGGS and GORDON SLATER.

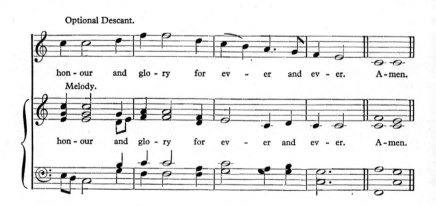

CHANTS

Single

1

Dr. Philip Hayes, 1738–97.

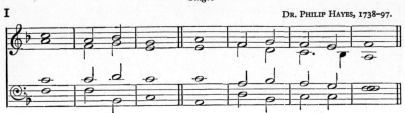

2

No. 12, Folk-Chant Book.

3

No. 44, Folk-Chant Book.

4

J. Battishill.

CHANTS
Single

5   Dr. W. Crotch.

6   R. Goodson.

7   Dr. T. S. Dupuis.

8   R. Farrant.

9   T. Purcell.

CHANTS
Single

10

Dr. Crotch.

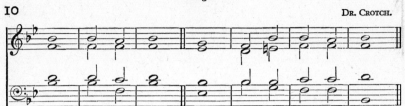

11

Burrowes.

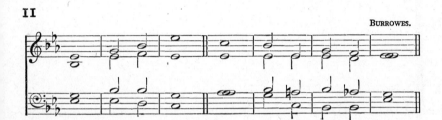

12

Dr. Cooke.

13

Adapted from Tonus Peregrinus.

14

Parisian Tone.

(219)

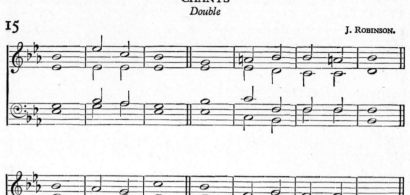

CHANTS
Double

15

J. ROBINSON.

16

T. NORRIS.

CHANTS
Double

INDEX OF MUSICAL SETTINGS
OF PRAYERS AND THANKSGIVINGS

(in alphabetical order)

For Index of Chants see overleaf.

INDEX OF CHANTS

Single

Double

247